DIVINE FEMININE ENERGY

HOW TO CONQUER YOUR FEARS AND FEELINGS OF ABANDONMENT, UNLEASH YOUR GODDESS ENERGY, DISCOVER YOUR TRUE SELF, AND BECOME AN IRRESISTIBLY ATTRACTIVE FORCE

KELLY COOPER

CONTENTS

Introduction   v

1. The Traits of the Divine Feminine   1
2. The Divine Feminine archetypes   19
3. The Scholar   27
4. The Maiden   33
5. The Adventurer   39
6. The Empress   43
7. The Creator   49
8. The Mother   53
9. The Priestess   57
10. The Hunter   63
11. The Rebel   69
12. The Lover   75
13. The Fae   81
14. The Friend   87
15. Next Steps   93
16. Reconciling with the Sacred Masculine   95
17. Utilising the Divine Feminine in Everyday Life   101
18. The Divine Feminine as Goddess Worship   111

Afterword   117

INTRODUCTION

WHAT IS THE DIVINE FEMININE?

The Divine Feminine is one half of the universal energy that creates and connects all things. Together with the Sacred Masculine, it is the source of all creation in the Universe and responsible for every atom, every star, every being in existence. The Divine Feminine and the Divine Masculine are the names we assign to the differing, sometimes contradictory nature of this Universal Energy in recognition of the dualistic nature of existence. When in harmony, the Divine Energies are capable of truly magnificent achievement, but when they are out of balance, the results can be stagnation and ennui, or at their worst, destructive.

The concept of the sacred feminine is nothing new, and shows up throughout world history in art, culture, and religion. Goddess worship was common in the past and continues around the world to this day. Our prehistoric ancestors moulded clay and carved stone into the stylized shape of women, with the "Venus of Hohle Fels" figurine – at the time of writing, the oldest known statuette of a full human - dating back over 35,000 years. The Uruk Vase, dating back to around 35000BCE, depicts the oldest known image of a god whom we can identify with certainty – the ancient Sumerian Goddess Inanna. Greece had Hera, Egypt had Isis, Babylon had Ishtar, and the Inca had Pachamamma to name but a few. In the modern world, the Hindus have Saraswati, Lakshmi and Parvati, the Buddhists have Tara, the Shintoists have Amerterasu, and in China, the ancient goddess Bixia Yuanjun is still worshipped by many.

In today's Western cultures, we have lost our connection to the Divine Feminine. Over the past thousand years, our society has increasingly given priority to the masculine while devaluing the feminine, the result of which has left many feeling out of balance and lost within themselves. Deep down, we all know something isn't quite right, because we are missing the connection to half of our divine selves. Since the 1800s, the women's rights movement has sought to address this by fighting for equality, accountability and protection for girls and women, and while their work is invaluable, alone it is not enough.

The systems we live under today are not the Divine Masculine; the lack of balance with the Feminine counterpart has led to a toxic system that hurts men just as much as it does women. Within our society, the Divine Masculine exists as his shadow self - aggressive, abusive, and controlling, seeking power and wealth for ego alone. In response, the Divine Feminine has retreated to her shadow side so that we now associate her key aspects in terms of weakness, manipulation, passiveness, and insecurity.

But how to address this? How do we bring out the strengths of the Divine Feminine, and reawaken the light in the Sacred Masculine, both within ourselves and in our society as a whole?

Simple. We must once again embrace the Divine Feminine as equal and integral to the Divine Masculine within ourselves, society, and the world. It is only through opening our eyes to the chaos around us and giving equal respect to the Feminine that we will be guided back to our true nature. We must start within ourselves and allow our light to grow and influence those around us.

It is already happening. Women and men the world over are acknowledging and honouring the Sacred Feminine in conjunction with the Masculine, and her return is the source of change and challenge to the restrictive systems that have hampered our society for so long.

THE DIVINE FEMININE IS NOT RESTRICTED BY BIOLOGY

The Feminine and the Masculine are not separate, distinct energies; rather, they exist in a symbiotic relationship that represents the duality of existence. This is well expressed by Chinese philosophy, where Yin and Yang are a balance between opposite ideals. The energies are not separate; the two shapes fit perfectly in an integrated whole, with the line between them a wave that allows them to flow with harmony, making room for more than one iteration of balance. There are many variations in the balance of these energies, and it is within this spectrum that we each seek our own equilibrium between the Masculine and the Feminine.

So it is within life itself. In our modern society we associate the Masculine with a narrow definition of being male, and the Feminine with the opposing, yet still narrow, definition of the female; definitions that have sadly been influenced by the imbalanced, shadow-Masculine world we have allowed to grow and suppress the optimal integration of both. We throw gendered insults at each other, and even as women as a group have fought to bring about equal rights in society, less attention has been given to the idea that the Feminine strengths are as valuable as the Masculine ones. We still prioritise the shadow-masculine ideals of aggression and wealth accumulation as evidence of "Strong Women", while the greatest qualities of the Divine Feminine – empathy, vulnerability, and gentleness, to name a few – are at best dismissed but often outright mocked as a weakness when displayed by men.

Across humanity there is a biological spectrum of physical traits, such as strength, height, flexibility, and so on. Men and women often fall into different, overlapping ranges when populations are categorized by their physicality, but it is important to understand that the Divine Feminine and Masculine are independent of physical characteristics. Even on a biological level, the variation in body chemistry, DNA, physical appearance, body parts and abilities are so broad that, while we can say men tend toward A and women tend toward B, there will always be exceptions that illustrate and celebrate the ways that the Universal Energies swirl and interact.

It is the same for our very nature and the aspects of the Sacred Energy that we express as individuals. Every living person is a blend of both the Divine Feminine and masculine, although the exact mix is unique to each of us. While scientific studies have shown that on a biological level there is no link between our brains and our gender identity, it is the cultures we are raised in that shapes whether we embrace the Feminine or the Masculine, and how we allow that Energy to manifest within us.

For the purposes of this book, we are concentrating on the Western interpretation of Masculine and Feminine, but remember that, depending on your own culture, life experience and childhood lessons, your understanding of the two energies may fall on a different place within the spectrum than others. This is something that is worth celebrating, for again, the two Sacred Energies are in a continuous interplay with each other, so there are infinite variations between the two. When we explore the Divine Feminine Archetypes keep in mind that although these figures represent ideas that span cultures and communities, it is your reaction to them – that is, whether you see them as positives or negatives – is the part of you where cultural learning can override your connection to the Divine. Pay attention to these feelings, question them and study them, for it is only through understanding that you can transcend your limitations and truly embrace your Divine self.

1

THE TRAITS OF THE DIVINE FEMININE

*I*f the Divine Feminine is the companion to the Divine Masculine, different but equal, what are the key aspects of her energy that we should be embracing rather than suppressing? What value lies in understanding and then encompassing these traits into ourselves?

INTUITION

Do you ever just know something is wrong about a situation, or just take an instant dislike to a person, and then later find out that your gut feeling saved you from a bad experience? What about the opposite? Have you ever had an opportunity that everyone told you was a bad thing, but that you knew deep down inside would change everything for the better? That's the Divine Feminine within you trying to manifest as Intuition.

In our masculine-dominated society, we prize Reason and Logic to such a degree that intuition has been relegated to the world of pseudoscience and irrational behaviour. In reality, intuition is a fundamental part of how humans make decisions, whether we acknowledge it or not, and many scientists regard intuition as a form of unconscious intelligence. They posit that a decision based on intuition can be just as rational as one based on Reason. Why? Because despite the popular idea of intuition being based on nothing but feelings, it actually incorporates a wealth of experience, pattern recognition and related knowledge that we access on a subconscious level. Intuition, then, is not the opposite of Reason, but rather a different approach to incorporating information.

This is not to say that the Feminine Energy of Intuition is superior to its twin Masculine Energy of Reason; it is easy to mistake our fears or arrogance for Intuition, or we can use it to make snap decisions before we have access to all the relevant information. At the same time, relying solely on Reason to the exclusion of Intuition is to deny ourselves the value of our personal experience and background knowledge. It can prevent us from making effective decisions in a timely manner, which is particularly damaging when time is of the essence. By embracing this facet of the Divine Feminine, we are able to make better decisions for ourselves and for others.

VULNERABILITY

Have you ever been in a situation where someone has hurt you, verbally or physically, but you hid your true feelings about the matter and pretended it was no big deal? Have you ever told a friend or family member about something you are truly passionate about, only to apologise for your enthusiasm because it feels childish to express your excitement? Do you admire people who can remain cool and detached in any scenario, even when they are facing public ridicule and mockery? Have you ever said or thought that boys and men shouldn't cry?

Embracing the Divine Feminine trait of Vulnerability involves a willingness to show others your wounds and failures while trusting that they will not use this knowledge to cause you harm. In modern society, men have been conditioned to believe that displaying

Vulnerability of any kind is a weakness and character flaw, while women are criticized for showing emotions as though it is something that needs to be fixed. Even healthy displays of emotion, such as crying over the death of a loved one, are subjected to criticism and review. Vulnerability does not apply solely to displays of painful emotions, such as sadness or even anger, but expressing true joy and enjoyment in things can incur equal amounts of censure and disdain from society, as it can be considered childish.

These societal attitudes are evidence that we have embraced the shadow side of the Divine Masculine trait of Impassiveness. We value the ability to remain dispassionate in all scenarios, teach our sons that crying is childish, and regard intense emotional reactions - both negative and positive - as something to be ashamed of. At the same time, we think of the Divine Feminine trait of Vulnerability in terms of victimhood, helplessness and hysteria – her shadow aspects.

Embracing the trait of vulnerability is to acknowledge that we are human. It is an integral part of building connections and relationships with others, and is the only path we have to finding lasting love and companionship. After all, if we wish to grow emotionally and psychologically, we must acknowledge our personal vulnerability and risk the pain that comes from those vulnerabilities. How can we love someone with all our heart, if we are not willing to risk our heart being broken?

EMPATHY

Have you ever listened to someone else's story, and found yourself crying for their pain, cheering for their success and experiencing embarrassment for their mistakes, even though you don't actually know them? This is a manifestation of the Divine Feminine Energy of Empathy, which grants us the ability to imagine what someone else might be thinking or feeling. Empathy also allows us to correctly sense and interpret the mood and feelings of the people around us, even when their actions and words contradict their emotions.

The Masculine Energy trait of Judgement has become increasingly prized in the modern world, where our society feels more comfortable by defining actions, and often individual people, as either Good or Bad, or Right versus Wrong. Because we all prefer to think of ourselves as good and honest people, we use Judgement in its shadow form to condemn others whose behaviour and beliefs differ from our own for no other reason than they are different from our own. In this context, Empathy can be seen as a betrayal of community or a rejection of tradition, and so is often dismissed as a weakness.

In reality, when the Divine Feminine Energy is embraced as Empathy, we are able to develop communication and understanding. It encourages us to listen to other perspectives and consider alternative points of view, which in turn can lead us to new ideas and innovations. Empathy teaches us to seek the reasons and explanations behind the actions and choices of others, and is essential to diplomacy and relationship-building at every level.

When out of balance with its Masculine counterpart, Empathy can lead to negative outcomes, such as an inability to make hard decisions, or a tendency to excuse poor choices and bad actions in others rather than seeking justice. It can also leave people susceptible to emotional manipulation if they are not able to easily separate their own emotions from those of the people around them.

By embracing the Divine Feminine trait of Empathy, we can improve our relationships on both a personal and societal level, while tempering it with the Masculine Energy of Judgement allows us to remain true to our own values and integrity.

CREATION

How do you express your inner creative? Do you play with traditional media like painting or sculpture? Have you embraced traditional women's crafts like knitting or embroidery? Perhaps your outlet is through food and creating new dishes for your loved ones to try. Do you write, even if no one reads it? Or is your creativity spilling out in your home, your garden, or the way you dress?

The Divine Feminine has always been tied to the act of creation, although somewhere in our culture's history, we began to devalue the concept until we formed the opinion that Science was not only in opposition to the Arts, and that the former was also superior. And then, within the Arts themselves, we established another hierarchy, where the mediums historically used by men – oil painting, sculpture, architecture, etc – were considered more worthy of notice and praise than the art forms more regularly employed by women – sewing, quilting, tapestry, and the like.

In the process of devaluing the Divine Feminine trait of Creation, we seem to have forgotten what it actually is. Although Art is a form of Creation, not all Creation is Art. Creation is the act of bringing something into existence, of forming something new from your dreams and imagination alone. Creation is the ultimate celebration of the Divine, and the most sacred way to access that part of ourselves.

Creation is found in every new solution to an existing problem. It is the driving force in science, where new experiments and theories are created as we seek to understand the world. It is found in the office and the workplace when the software developer writes new code, or the administrator builds a new spreadsheet. Every meal we cook is an act of creation, as is every building that we construct, and every house that we turn into a home. Our children are the living embodiment of creation, not just from their parents, but from our whole society as we create the next generation of adults to continue what we have begun.

Without Creation there is no innovation, and while some parts of culture have embraced this Divine Feminine trait with abandon, there are others who cling to the Divine Masculine trait of Tradition instead, and remain suspicious of the change that Creation brings in her wake.

As with all traits, they have a shadow side. Tradition is the continuation of established patterns of thought, action, or behaviour, many of which exist because time and experience have shown them to be effective and useful. An example would be our road system; tradition dictates that having designated roadways is a good idea, so we accept it rather than embracing Creation and ripping up the old street system to replace it with a new one. But when in shadow, Tradition can become oppressive and restrictive, preventing us from learning new and better ways to be and do for no other reason than "we've always done it like this".

Equally, Creation for the sake of Creation is not always appropriate. There are often valid reasons for the existence of Traditional systems, so replacing them for no other reason than wanting something new often ends in destruction. Equally, the purpose and consequences of Creation can prove to be damaging; systems designed to harm or exclude certain groups, weapons and tools that serve no purpose but inflicting pain, or items that involve the destruction and poisoning of essential resources in their Creation are all examples of this trait in shadow.

When embracing your Divine Feminine trait of Creation, it is important to understand your motivation behind the act, and to make your decisions accordingly. Creation is your gift to the world, and the way we leave our legacies behind. Make them good ones.

NURTURE

Is there a time in your life that you were cared for, protected, encouraged and guided as you grew and developed as a person? Are you the one who provides, or have provided, that support to another person? In popular culture, we associate the Divine Feminine trait of Nurture with an idealised mother figure; a woman whose role is to keep you safe when you are at your weakest, and who provides the supports you require to become the best version of yourself. Fathers, siblings, friends, teachers, partners and business associates are all capable of manifesting this trait, as Nurture is independent of gender, familial ties or social status.

The Divine Feminine trait of Nurture is often undervalued and dismissed by our society, where it is conflated with infantilizing and coddling people. We expect people to "toughen up" or "grow a thick skin" if our criticism hurts them or dismiss potentially traumatic experiences as being "character building". We obsess over forcing people "out of their comfort zone" regardless of whether they are ready to face difficult situations, because we have bought into the belief that growth and development only happen when we are uncomfortable, despite all evidence to the contrary.

The Divine Masculine trait that pairs with Nurture is Authority; that is, the belief that someone else knows what is best for you/you know what is best for another person, so that an individual's personal feelings, interests and experiences are things to be overcome rather than acknowledged. When undertaken in the light, Authority helps people to move past challenges they find overwhelming or allows a group to function effectively in complex scenarios. In shadow, however, it prioritises the opinions of the Authority Figure over the individual, leaving them at risk of abuse, manipulation and depression.

When manifesting the Divine Feminine trait of Nurture, our role is to provide those in our care – including ourselves – the right environment. A seed won't sprout just because you ordered it to do so; it needs the right soil, the right amount of water, and the right amount of light if you want it to grow. Equally, the conditions one plant needs to flourish will cause another plant to die; Nurture is about creating the create environment for the things we are caring for and understanding that each situation may require a different set of tools.

In order to truly embrace the Divine Feminine trait of Nurture, however, it is important that we first try to nurture ourselves. In a world where we are expected to be constantly productive, it can be difficult to step back and make time to rest and recuperate. Only you know what your perfect environment looks like, and it may take time for you to build it, but learning to nurture yourself will help you learn how to nurture others.

COMPASSION

When you see someone suffering or in trouble, do you experience a desire to help fix the problem, or at least ease their pain in whatever way you can? That feeling is the manifestation of the Divine Female Trait of Compassion. Where Empathy allows us to connect and understand the experiences of another, Compassion is the desire to help make things better.

Embracing the Divine Feminine Trait of Compassion involves leaving our comfort zone and working for the good of another person or group, with no thought of benefit for ourselves. It is the most altruistic of all the Feminine traits, and when done in Light, it is a powerful tool for Good in the world. Compassion is how we build a just, fair world, because it is about acting on the impulse to fix injustice. This might be as simple as taking circumstances into account before making a judgement, as small as making a coffee for a stressed-out co-worker, or as intense as providing free labour or services for those in need. There are women and men in this world whose Compassion is so pure that they have dedicated their lives to resolving injustice or helping those in most need. Compassion is what makes us human.

When in shadow, however, Compassion can lead to arrogance, moral superiority, and paternalism. In our modern world, you can see this in attempts to fix societal issues such as addiction and homelessness; for example, the assumption that all addicts are non-functional and take drugs due to a moral failing, therefore limiting their access to vital supports such as housing, medical services and counselling unless they are clean. While the people trying to help might well be operating from a place of Compassion – they genuinely care and want to help – they are working from shadow, where they are assuming that they understand the situation better than anyone else, and are receiving self-gratification for being a "Good Person". On an international scale, the shadow side of Compassion can show up in Relief efforts, where agencies turn up to deliver the services they specialise in without any real understanding of what is actually needed by the people on the ground.

The twin Divine Masculine trait that pairs with Compassion is Dispassion. When used in Light, Dispassion allows us to assess situations without letting our emotions and biases blind us to the truth, and is essential when it comes to assessing the effectiveness of ideas or solutions. Unfortunately, our modern society has elevated the shadow side of Dispassion to the status of a virtue, perpetuating the idea that decisions should be made in a cold, logical fashion with no thought to their potential human cost. Thus we see Compassion as a weakness, as though caring for the fate of others and wanting to help fix problems that are causing harm to real people is something we should be ashamed of. We mock those who care about the unfortunate, the destitute, the environment, or wildlife, calling them "bleeding hearts" for wanting the world to be better for everyone. While yes, some of these individuals are operating in the shadow side of Compassion and we might not all agree on solutions, their connection to the Divine Feminine is something to be celebrated and embraced rather than ridiculed.

FORGIVENESS

Can you think of a time when you or someone you know failed in some way, but the major cause of their upset was the feeling they had "let everyone down"? Perhaps they were in competitive sports, and a mistake cost them a medal. Maybe they were laid off from their job and were scared for the future. It could have been the betrayal of a confidence or a failed examination. The common denominator in all these situations is the feeling that their failure was a result of a personal flaw, and that it could have been avoided if only they'd tried harder in some unspecified way.

The Divine Feminine trait of Forgiveness is in danger of becoming a lost art in our society, for her shadow version has felt increasingly dominant over the last few decades. We treat forgiveness as a gift we bestow upon others, often stating "I forgive you" to people before they apologise in a misguided attempt at proving that we are enlightened people. Equally, if someone offers an apology our default is to expect it to be accepted and forgiveness granted no matter the issue, even to the extent that we will criticize and condemn anyone who will not perform the act of public forgiveness for the good of the group. It's no wonder, then, that we've lost touch with the true power of this trait and what it means to manifest it.

To truly embody the Divine feminine trait of Forgiveness, we must first forgive ourselves for being human. We are naturally flawed, complex creatures who are easily impacted by environmental factors and whose Will, no matter how strong, is not unbreakable. While we are so often pushed to be perfect, we are incapable of being infallible. Despite knowing this, we still try, telling ourselves that so long as we put in 110%, it's okay, because we were perfect in our attitude and attempt. Even then we will fail because we won't always try our best or our hardest; it is just not possible to operate at maximum effectiveness twenty-four hours a day, seven days a week; even machines need time for maintenance.

Our society rewards success and sneers at failure, but its most damaging habit is the way it condemns mediocrity. It is not enough to be ordinary; one must strive for the extraordinary. It is not acceptable to live a good life; it must be your best life. This is damaging us on many levels, and ignores the fundamental truth that it our flaws and mistakes that make us human. Instead, we lean hard into the Divine Masculine trait of Discipline, convincing ourselves that we can overcome any limitation through sheer hard work, and that so long as we keep fighting no matter what, our success is guaranteed. This shadow aspect of Discipline convinces us that any failure is actually a moral failure, and that if only we'd worked harder, we could have been perfect.

By manifesting Forgiveness for ourselves by acknowledging we are imperfect by nature, it makes it easier to find forgiveness for others, and to help them forgive themselves. It helps us temper our expectations and to better understand ourselves, but most importantly it leads to us bringing more good into the world with the realisation that perfection is not always necessary.

It is important to recognise that Forgiveness is not a gift to be bestowed on another, nor is it something than should be demanded or expected. Equally, Forgiveness does not negate the need for atonement. Pressuring another person into forgiving another is a shadow act of manipulation and as reprehensible as wielding Forgiveness like a bargaining chip. There are actions and crimes that some people consider unforgiveable, and it is their right to choose not to forgive the person that wronged them. Culturally we have this idea that forgiving those who have hurt you will grant you peace; this is not true for everyone, and it is against the Divine Feminine to push another person to forgive if they do not wish to. The trait of Forgiveness does not demand that you forgive a deliberate act of pain or violence, but rather that you acknowledge our inherent imperfections and understand that mistakes are part of the human experience.

INNOCENCE

Do you remember a time when the world was full of potential and wonder? A time when you felt safe pursuing every shiny thing that caught your attention, that every path could lead to a fabulous new adventure, and that your future was pure potential? This is the manifestation of the Divine Feminine state of Innocence.

The Divine Feminine trait of Innocence is more than freedom from guilt or sin; it is a state of curiosity and wonder that is untainted by knowledge of evil and negativity. When manifesting Innocence, we see the best in the people around us and the opportunity in every challenge. We are overflowing with potential, and are unburdened by responsibility, consequence and knowledge. So many times people impose limits on themselves because they believe something to be impossible, only for another to come along and prove those limits to be false as they smash through them. Innocence allows us to experience sheer joy in each moment without fear that we will be mocked or criticized. It enables us to explore and ask questions unburdened with the worry of being thought ignorant or stupid. We can meet people and accept them for who they are now without judgement based on rumour and gossip.

When in shadow, Innocence can become ignorance. In this state, people feel a sense of superiority in their lack of knowledge, and resist the need for education or exploration. The Divine Feminine trait of Innocence is not about constructs such as purity, but rather about the acceptance of how vast the Universe is, how diverse the human experience is, and being excited by the possibilities that represents.

The Divine Masculine trait that twins with Innocence is Experience. When manifested in the light, Experience is essential to our growth and our survival, for it is how we learn that fire burns us, but there are ways to harness that power for our benefit. It teaches us that not everyone is good, and that we need to prepare for bad things so that we can thrive in any circumstance. When in shadow, Experience becomes hoarded knowledge and is used to belittle and dismiss the thoughts of those without it. It quickly sinks into ennui and the idea that enthusiasm is naïve ignorance, while being jaded and disaffected demonstrates sophistication.

To manifest the Divine Feminine trait of Innocence in yourself, let go of your own judgement and allow yourself to find joy in small things. Allow yourself to become ridiculously excited about something you enjoy. Admit to knowing nothing about a topic that nonetheless interests you, and learn. Encourage others to share their unbridled enthusiasm for their interests with you, even if it not a passion you share. Commit to becoming a cheerleader rather than a dream-killer, both for others and for yourself.

REFLECTION

There is an old adage that states insanity is doing the same thing over and over again, but expecting different results. There has been a moment in everyone's life where we have struggled to complete a task, and grown increasingly frustrated as we try over and over again to succeed, and yet get no closer to the goal.

The Divine Feminine trait of Reflection is the act of taking a step back from a situation to analyse it from other angles. It involves serious thought and consideration of an issue or task, with the goal of coming to an effective conclusion or resolution. To truly manifest Reflection, opposing or contradictory views must be taken into consideration even if they are quickly dismissed; Reflection is not about snap judgements, but rather an exploration of all options. When manifested in light, Reflection allows us to break out of destructive cycles and find real solutions to the problems we face, saving us time, effort and considerable frustration.

When in shadow, however, Reflection can be used to excuse a lack of progress and procrastination. It can lead to "analysis paralysis", which occurs when there are too many options or too much information to allow for timely decisions. It can cost us opportunities and experiences if we dither too much, wasting time and resources in the process.

In contrast, the Masculine Energy trait of Action is the impetus behind implementing steps or solutions. When manifested in light, Action pushes us to make decisions in a timely manner and do the work necessary to achieve the results that we need. When in shadow, Action drives us to leap without looking, to make mistakes that could have easily been avoided with a moment of reflection, make rash choices, or get stuck in a never-ending cycle of doing the same thing over and over again without achieving results.

In order to manifest the Divine Feminine Energy of Reflection, take the time to look at the problems and roadblocks in your life, and the actions that have failed to remove them. Consider alternative options and solutions, and commit to taking just a moment of Reflection before making decisions.

GENTLENESS

Have you ever held a small animal in your hands and felt how fragile its life was as it wriggled on your palm? A tiny chick, maybe, or a lizard, or a hamster. What about holding a newborn infant in your arms, when you're careful to support their little heads and they stare up at you with wide, trusting eyes? Has there been a time when you've had to take care of someone in distress, where you spoke softly, and kindly, and helped them to stay calm in a stressful situation?

The Divine Feminine trait of Gentleness allows us to walk softly in the world, it is the source of our kindness and our ability to take care of fragile things. Gentleness allows us to both appreciate and experience the beauty of the delicate and grants us the understanding that a soft approach is as valuable in the world as a hard one.

Gentleness balances the Divine Masculine of Strength, which is why it is so often mistaken for its shadow form of weakness. In our society, we prioritize Strength in its shadow form, where it too easily slips into brutality. We need Strength to help us make hard decisions and to stand up in the face of injustice, and can manifest it in our bodies as a way to better move through the world. By contrast, we manifest Gentleness in those situations where a light touch is more effective, and even the physically strongest people among us can hold a fragile newborn without hurting them.

In her shadow form, Gentleness can manifest as learned helplessness. This is when we choose not to help ourselves in difficult situations, or rely on others to "save" us when we are capable of fixing the problem at hand. This should not be confused with an inability to help ourselves; sadly, there are dark places in our existence where victims cannot break free without help from the outside. Rather, it is knowing that you are capable of walking a difficult road to escape, but choosing to wait for someone to come and carry you instead.

It is often far more difficult and time-consuming to choose Gentleness and kindness as an approach, but when used correctly, it allows fragile, complex, and truly world-changing beauty to flourish and grow within its touch.

SENSUALITY

The idea of Sensuality has become intertwined with sexuality in our modern world, when this Divine Feminine trait encompasses so much more. While the physical connection between consenting adults is one manifestation of Sensuality, in her purest form, she is about stimulation for all our senses.

When you embrace the Divine Feminine Trait of Sensuality, you acknowledge the visceral pleasure of existence. You notice and react to changes in your environment, becoming aware of both delicate scents and intense smells, and the impact they have on your emotional state. Our eyes are attuned to both the beautiful and the repulsive, our ears recognising both discordance and harmony. We appreciate the way certain materials feel on our skin, and are aware of how the environment around us – temperature, air pressure, humidity – impacts both our bodies and our minds. In terms of intimate experience, we engage all our senses and are confident in our own preferences while respecting those of others. We are sensitive to the smallest changes in the environment and the people around us, and can use these insights to help us move through the world.

In shadow, Sensuality can manifest as indulgence, where we seek only pleasure for our own sake, caring little if anything for the impact our choices have on the world, or whether our actions are pleasurable for those around us. In this context, indulgence is a selfish act that focuses in on the experience of pleasure dissociated from the rest of our inner self, and ultimately disconnects us from the full range of sensual experience the world contains.

In the Divine Masculine, Restraint is the twin to Sensuality. Restraint manifests in the acknowledgement that sensory overload can be overwhelming, or to put it simply, that it's possible to have too much of a good thing. Restraint also allows us to avoid temptation when other responsibilities demand our attention, and helps us to retain composure when emotions and other sensations threaten to overwhelm us. In the shadow form, however, Restraint can manifest as Denial, both as punishment to the self and to others, when a deliberate choice to withhold pleasurable experiences is made. This can lead to damaging associations between pleasure and shame, which ultimately disconnects us from the full range of sensual experience in much the same way that Indulgence can do.

When building your connection with the Divine Feminine trait of Sensuality, remember that our senses exist to help us experience and navigate the world. Paying attention to the emotions they invoke will heighten your intuition and understanding of both yourself and your relationships.

REBELLION

Does the idea of injustice make you angry? How many times in your life have you encountered an invisible boundary put in place by the powerful, and felt the urge to tear it down? Have you been forced to play by the rules of those in charge, laughing along at their jokes while secretly wanting to set the whole building on fire? Have you ever protested, signed petitions, campaigned for change, or just stood up for another person and said out loud, "this is wrong"?

This is the manifestation of the Divine Feminine trait of Rebellion as it fights to be heard. Rebellion is our reaction to injustice and our desire to create a fairness in a world where most of the power rests in the hands of a select few. In our society we are taught to "go along to get along," and have been conditioned to turn a blind eye to systems that we know are unfair. These very systems are also designed to punish those who speak out against them, meaning that the vast majority of us have learned to suppress our desire to rebel in favour of the Divine Masculine trait of Conformity.

When operating in the light, Conformity allows us to establish communities with shared ideals, and to build societies – both physically and intellectually – that have the standards, laws and infrastructure needed for its members to thrive. It lets everyone know what is expected both from them and of others in their community, so that everyone has their basic needs met. When operating in shadow, however, Conformity becomes a weapon of stagnation, and a tool to keep wealth in the hands of the powerful. Societal expectations of behaviour stop being about protecting the vulnerable, and instead become a way to punish those who question the way things are done.

Of all the Divine Feminine traits, Rebellion is perhaps the hardest to embody. Whether it is challenging a restrictive work rule or threatening an unjust law of the nation, Rebellion puts us into the view of people who benefit from the status quo, which can threaten many aspects of our life. Even when rebelling against seemingly small injustices, such as challenging an inappropriate joke from a family member, the fallout for the rebel can feel disproportionately painful considering the nature of their challenge.

And yet without Rebellion, we would never experience societal change. Serfdom and slavery would still be the bedrock of our society, and the richest would be able to exploit the poorest far worse than they do at present. It was the Rebels of all backgrounds who fought for freedom, equality, equitability, worker rights, consumer protections, and accountability regardless of wealth. It is the highest manifestation of the Divine Feminine to Rebel against injustice, no matter how difficult it may be on a personal level.

Rebellion, like all other Divine traits, has a shadow side, and this is rebelling for the sake of it. Not all systems are broken, and Conformity is not always wrong. The "Rebels without a cause" are coming from a place of selfishness and a desire for individual attention regardless of the cost or harm it causes, and their acts of defiance can be viewed as a desire to be superior to those around them.

When manifesting the Divine Feminine trait of Rebellion, remember that the source of this energy should be a desire to make the world a more equitable place, not to be lauded as a hero or leader. It can be frightening to stand against authority, especially when you stand alone, but without people willing to challenge injustice, nothing will ever change.

2

THE DIVINE FEMININE ARCHETYPES

*N*ow that we have learned about the traits embodied by the Divine Feminine, it is time to explore her archetypes, and introduce ways to use them in your quest to regain your connection to her power. While the Archetypes themselves are used to represent a universal experience that is independent of our culture, for the purposes of this book, their names are chosen with regard to the Western tradition. If they do not fit with your personal experience or cultural understanding, then please feel free to choose alternative names that have relevance for you.

Archetypes are universal, inborn models of behaviours and personalities that influence how we interact with the world. It is theorised that archetypes are representations of the ancestral memories and knowledge that were passed down to us from our ancestors. They embody our innate ways of being, our default settings if you will, and it is our life experiences that determine which of these archetypes we most embody.

As discussed earlier, the Divine Masculine dominates our society and thus ourselves, and he has slipped into his shadow form as the Divine Feminine has been repressed. As a result we are all restricted by the extremes of Shadow Masculine thinking and ideals, meaning we have lacked access to positive models and embodiments of Feminine Light. Through studying and understanding the nature of the archetypes contained in this book, we will learn how to identify their powers and traits within ourselves, and begin to redress this energy imbalance. With time we can harness the traits of both the Divine Feminine and Masculine, and become the integrated, powerful beings that we all have the potential to be.

Here we are exploring the twelve Divine Feminine archetypes and the parts of ourselves that they represent. Each of us is a unique soul with distinct psychological and emotional systems that enable us to make sense of reality. Regardless of gender, we all carry a complex mosaic of both Divine Masculine and Divine Feminine Archetypes within our personalities. These archetypal energies dance and intertwine within us, presenting as unique personalities and ways of experiencing the world. Where some of us see beauty, others see vulgarity, and where some perceive risk, others find adventure. Studying the Divine Feminine archetypes allows us a window into our own nature as well as the nature of those around us. By learning to access and express their energies alongside the Divine Masculine archetypes we already embody, we will take a significant step toward harmonious balance within ourselves.

HOW TO USE THE ARCHETYPES TO RECONNECT TO THE DIVINE FEMININE

Take the time to carefully read through and contemplate the description of each Archetype, paying close attention to your initial reaction to her. If possible, grab a notebook to keep beside you as you make your way through this section of the book, noting down your thoughts and feelings as you read. Consider the following questions:

- How would you summarise this archetype?

- What is your initial emotional reaction to her? Does that change with further contemplation?
- In what ways are you currently embodying her? Is she in light or in shadow?
- Where do you feel you need to nurture her further?
- How would it impact your life to embody her in different scenarios?
- What scares you about integrating her into your life further?
- How would it feel to manifest her fully?

Studying each Archetype in turn, compare her against the Divine Feminine traits and consider how, and to what extent, she embodies each. Contemplate and record the ways in which each combination could manifest in your daily life, and note down any examples where this has already happened for you. Take the time to reflect on how you would feel should you witness the manifestation of each combination; frightened? Powerful? Frustrated? Repeat for each Archetype until you have cycled through all twelve.

Choose the Archetype that intrigues you the most. Meditate on her meaning, and on both the light and shadow versions of her nature. Find a picture that best represents the Archetype for you, and place it beside your bed or beneath your pillow as you sleep. Pay attention to your dreams and make note of any sensations or experiences that are stirred within your subconscious. Repeat with each Archetype until you have cycled through all twelve.

As an extension of the above exercise, repeat the process but this time, pair the Archetype with one of her sisters. Explore how their different natures intertwine in both positive and negative ways. Are there instances in your life where two archetypes are pulling you in different directions, and if so, how can you reconcile this duality?

Or would embodying the energy of a second Archetype bolster and strengthen the powers of the first?

Identify an area in your life where you feel lacking; it could be your career, your romantic relationships, your financial situation, or anything that is causing you to worry. Define this issue clearly in your notebook, being specific about the nature of the problem. For example, if you are unhappy in your current relationship, state clearly, "I feel disconnected from my spouse", or "My partner and I argue almost daily", or "I am unfulfilled when it comes to intimacy". Next, imagine that you have manifested each of the archetypes in her full glory, unrestrained by the influence of the others. Ask yourself how you would respond to the question when in this state of power and write down your answer. Repeat with each Archetype, and then review the responses. If one resonates with you stronger than the others, then revisit that Archetype and explore the options open through her when she is integrated with her Divine counterparts.

At all stages of this process, pay attention to your feelings toward each Archetype and whether you are particularly drawn or repulsed by any of them. When this happens it is best to pause in your study and take the time to explore those emotions to uncover what it is that is causing the reaction – are you drawn to one card because she is familiar and comfortable, or because she represents what you wish to be? Are you repulsed because society has taught you to see her only in shadow, or because the idea of embracing her power is intimidating? Remember, the purpose of the archetypes is to aid you in your quest to connect with the Feminine Divine, which means they are a tool to help explore the hidden and neglected parts of your nature. Trust yourself, and let your soul be your own guide.

A SUMMARY OF THE DIVINE FEMININE ARCHETYPES

THE SCHOLAR represents a love of learning, inquiry, and knowledge. She seeks to understand both people and the Universe and is excited by any opportunity to learn and improve.

THE MAIDEN represents youthful innocence, curiosity, and implicit trust. She sees her home as a place full of potential and wonders, just waiting to be found.

THE ADVENTURER represents the burning desire to find out where each new path might lead. She hungers for new places to explore and new things to experience beyond her current understanding.

THE EMPRESS represents a desire for order and control. She prefers to lead from the front rather than relying on others and will do everything in her power to protect those she is responsible for.

THE CREATOR represents a need to make something from nothing, to innovate and create new things, theories and ideas. She sees potential in everything and is not afraid to try out new and radical approaches

THE MOTHER represents kindness and nurturing. Her focus is on providing care and support for those around her, and she willingly puts her own interests aside when others are in need

THE PRIESTESS represents the need for self-determination. She views power over our own fate and own nature as the highest expression of Sacred Ideals.

THE HUNTER represents a willingness to provide protection for others. She has mastered the skills needed to survive and thrive but turns them toward helping others instead of enriching herself.

THE REBEL represents the desire to challenge the status quo. She is willing to stand up for her beliefs even when they make her unpopular and will not accept tradition for tradition's sake alone.

THE LOVER represents a need for human connection and the power of desire. She embraces the sensual and sexual aspects of her nature and will use them in pursuit of her goals.

THE FAE represents playfulness and abandon. She is a trickster who delights in pranks and the absurd, as laughter and joy are integral to her existence

THE FRIEND represents consistency and reliability. She is the embodiment of belonging and will always be there to support and cheer for the people in her circle.

THE POSITIONS OF THE ARCHETYPES

If you wish to truly engage with the archetypes to fully manifest your Divine Feminine power, then it is important to understand the position they occupy in your psyche. This is not the same as being in light or shadow – it is about the degree to which you are channelling their energy on either a conscious or subconscious level.

Archetype in Dominance

When an archetype is in dominance, you will embody her in both attitude and behaviour, while her traits will guide your decision-making process. An archetype may be in dominance for short periods of time, for example during a stressful situation, or she may represent your default personality. With practice, you can learn to manifest specific archetypes in dominance to help you manage your daily life and to become your best self.

Archetype in Influence

When an archetype is in influence, you may not be directly manifesting her traits and powers, but her nature will be adjusting the behaviour of the archetype in dominance on either a conscious or subconscious level. This can be pronounced, or it can be subtle, but it is important to be aware that are Archetypes are rarely manifested in isolation, and that they will modify the traits of one another.

Think of Archetypes in influence as a support team for whoever is in dominance; when manifest in light they provide additional tools and perspectives, or act as counterbalance to a dominant archetype in shadow. When in shadow themselves, archetypes in influence can represent self-sabotage and damaging default behaviours that can undo the good work of the dominant archetype, or take a dominant archetype in shadow to some very dark places indeed.

Archetype in Submission

When an archetype is in submission, you are suppressing her traits and tendencies in situations where she could be of use to you. While this can be done on both a conscious and subconscious level, placing an Archetype into submission is not a neutral act, but an active one. The archetype in submission represents the path not taken and the choice not made. If you find that you are consistently placing the same archetypes into submission, then it is time to revisit her and ask yourself why.

The contradiction inherent in this position, however, is that despite being placed in a subservient role, this archetype is still wielding influence over your life. Whether that manifests as a refusal to act in a certain way or the feeling that her strengths would not help in certain situations, it is important to remember that it normal and even beneficial to have an archetype in submission, so long as it is not a permanent act, even when they are in shadow.

3

THE SCHOLAR

The Scholar believes in the power of information and the sheer joy of acquiring knowledge. She is never happier than when she is surrounded by books, magazines, journals, or any other media that feeds her desire to learn. She navigates the world by using her intellect and analytical mind, and is often considered a genius by the other Archetypes. In truth, she is not so much a natural genius as she is someone who knows there is always something to learn, and who excels at synthesizing new information. While she is well read on a wide range of topics, the Scholar finds no greater joy than taking a deep dive into her favourite subject areas. Her creativity is fuelled and shaped by her research, meaning she will not waste time chasing an option that experts have deemed impossible, but instead identify new paths to follow instead.

The Scholar believes that knowledge will lead to truth, and that there is no problem that cannot be overcome with the correct application of research, informed experimentation, and analysis. She sees knowledge and truth as the path to ultimate freedom, and values expertise over intuition.

She will rarely embark on an activity without fully understanding what it involved, and even then, she will take time to identify the best way to undertake something new before committing herself. This is not to say that she expects perfection from any undertaking; the Scholar understands that experiments will sometimes fail, and that a beginner will rarely outperform a master, but she knows that the data gleaned from such failure is essential for progress toward success.

The Scholar's never-ending pursuit of knowledge and information is not always in her best interest. It is not unusual for her to become so engrossed in her research and study that she neglects her relationships, or miss out on fun activities. When struggling with complex topics or difficult decisions, the Scholar can use research as a way to procrastinate, or may suffer from "analysis paralysis", where information overwhelm can stop her from making a decision. She is always more likely to over-research a problem than under-research it, so when she does give her opinion or make a decision, you can be sure that the Scholar has taken all known positions into account.

The value that the Scholar places on knowledge and information can lead to some finding her prosy and dull. She prefers not to idly speculate on any topic, and will happily correct anyone she thinks is misinformed. She does not suffer those she perceives as fools, and has little time for anyone who cannot back up their claims with hard evidence. By contrast, the Scholar values the opinions of experts, and can even be deferential to those considered leaders in their field.

THE SCHOLAR IN RELATIONSHIPS

The scholar believes in judging people by both their actions and their words, so tends to be very selective about who she spends her time with. She strives to surround herself with interesting, intelligent people who can challenge her intellectually, or with those who are willing and able to learn from her.

In romantic relationships, the Scholar embodies the analytical approach to finding love. She has already weighed and considered potential partners against her well-researched list of ideal traits, and will not pursue or engage with anyone she feels cannot meet her requirements. On the other hand, when the Scholar meets her ideal match, she will be devoted to them – so long as they are her intellectual equal. If not careful, she can lapse into hero-worshipping and put her own pursuits second to those of her partner, especially if she considers them to be more intelligent that herself.

While the Scholar might not be the greatest friend when you are an emotional crisis, she excels at helping people out of bad situations and helping them reach their goals. She will demonstrate her love by researching and gathering information on behalf of those important to her, and is always willing to share her skills and knowledge for their benefit. While she has no time for anyone she regards as wallowing or willfully ignorant, so long as a person is trying to solve their problems, she will be there to lend a hand.

THE SCHOLAR IN SHADOW

When in Shadow, the Scholar's focus on knowledge and information can lead her to be arrogant and opinionated. This is particularly evident on subjective matters, where she will insist that her opinion is the only true and correct one, while barraging her opponent with irrelevant data and statistics.

At her worst, the Scholar in Shadow's arrogance will lead her to discount any knowledge or evidence that runs against her own beliefs, because it is impossible for her to ever admit that she could draw an incorrect conclusion. She will force the facts to fit her narrative, no matter how outlandish her ideas become in the process.

That is not to suggest that everything about the Scholar in Shadow is a negative; she reminds us that sometimes you have to have faith in what you know to be true, even when the world is telling you otherwise. The Scholar in Shadow knows she is right and is willing to prove it despite popular opinion, which has led to many great breakthroughs and discoveries over the centuries.

THE SCHOLAR IN DOMINANCE

When you manifest the Scholar in dominance, your idea of heaven will probably be an infinite private library full of reading nooks and fresh notebooks. There is so much to learn and discover about every imaginable topic, that it's almost depressing to know that it's impossible for any one person to know everything there is to know.

The Scholar will lead you to a love of books, information and research, providing you with an appreciation of experts, academics, and master craftspeople. She will remind you that there is value in learning just for the sake of learning, and that all decisions should be made on a solid foundation of quality research.

THE SCHOLAR IN INFLUENCE

When in Influence, the Scholar tempers the nature of the other Archetypes by reminding them to consult the evidence before making their decisions. She encourages them to analyse data and understand the information before them, so that they can be confident in their decision. If the Archetype in Dominance is doubting themselves, the Scholar is there to prove to provide the proof they need to continue with confidence.

THE SCHOLAR IN SUBMISSION

When you push the Scholar into Submission, you are choosing to prioritise emotional choices to the exclusion of reason and wisdom.

This is not about trusting your gut instinct, but rather deliberately ignoring every red flag or warning sign before you in favour of optimism and blind faith. While this occasionally pays off, long term suppression of the Scholar suggests that you are ignoring the evidence before you as a way to avoid an unpleasant truth.

4

THE MAIDEN

The Maiden is young, playful, and full of innocent curiosity about the world. She believes life is full of unlimited opportunity, and believes that no matter how bad things get, they will always work out for the best. She is uncorrupted by experience, and so her faith and optimism make her willing to take risks and try new things. Because of this, the Maiden is often creative, but not necessarily talented. This does not bother her, however, because what matters most is the new experience.

While the maiden is open to new opportunities, she does not go for looking for them. She tends to choose her path by whim rather than having a set direction and can be easily distracted by something new or interesting. She rarely commits to anything long term and is prone to choosing instant gratification over future results. The maiden isn't one to make plans, and she can happily put off anything she finds dull or boring to a future date.

The Maiden's curiosity and innocence, however, can have negative consequences. While she may be brimming with ideas and optimism, she lacks the follow-through necessary to make progress on any of them. Her habit of putting off unpleasant tasks in favour of fun can cause her significant problems in all aspects of her life, from financial troubles to an inability to hold down a job long term. The Maiden is not the most reliable of people, either; because she is both impulsive and easily distracted, it is not unusual for her to cancel plans at the last minute because an opportunity came her way that she simply had to explore.

The maiden's lack of knowledge about worldly issues can lead some to find her boring, or her understanding of complex topics quite shallow. This may lead them to dismiss her as stupid or uneducated, when this is rarely the case: the Maiden is aware that there is much she doesn't know, and is always happy to be taught more on topics that capture her fancy, but her butterfly nature and perpetual optimism make it hard to take her opinion seriously.

Her naivety about the darker side of the world puts the Maiden at risk of being manipulated or hurt by others, or being taken advantage of. As such, it is not unusual to find a self-appointed protector in her orbit. This could be a family member, friend, or romantic partner who spends a lot of their energy trying to temper her impulses, clean up any messes, and explaining that life involves doing boring or distasteful chores just as much as the fun stuff.

THE MAIDEN IN RELATIONSHIPS

One of the Maiden's key strengths is her willingness to accept others at face value, and a determination to like everyone. Her happy-go-lucky attitude to life makes her an easy companion, while her live-and-let-live approach to life make her naturally inclusive and friendly to all. She loves learning about new people and is genuinely interested in finding out more about them. She truly wants everyone around her to be happy, and will happily cheer on anyone trying to achieve their dreams, even if it's not something she's personally interested in. These traits make her a desirable friend for many, no matter their own social status.

In relationships, the Maiden embodies the first blush of romantic love, where everything seems perfect between you, and you are constantly discovering new, wonderful things. The Maiden gives freely from her heart, body, and soul, for she is not burdened by the shame and doubt that has been piled on her by societal expectations. When she falls in love the Maiden falls fast and deep, for the excitement of a new relationship can be intoxicating for her.

Unfortunately, the Maiden can be something of a fair-weather friend, and is unlikely to remain in a relationship for long. While she would never intentionally harm another person, she lacks the maturity and experience to understand that her impulsiveness can be deeply hurtful, or that her unreliability can cause stress for others. Because her own nature is to see the positives in everything, she has very little time for people who are jaded or pessimistic, even when they have every right to be. She would rather run away and forget about problems than have hard or difficult conversations, which is why most of her relationships are short-lived or only surface level.

THE MAIDEN IN SHADOW

When in Shadow, the Maiden's innocent curiosity turns into helplessness. She is the stereotypical Damsel in Distress, whose naivety has drawn her into a dangerous situation, where she waits for someone else to come and rescue her.

The Maiden in Shadow is characterised by inaction under pressure. She expects that others will keep her safe, and so her behaviours can border on reckless. When the Maiden in Light uses her optimism to seek solutions to any problems she encounters, the Maiden in Shadow chooses to wait until someone else comes along to fix her mess. She feels the same desire for new experiences as her counterpart in light, but expects someone else to do all the hard work in planning and arranging things on her behalf.

Despite these negative traits, there is one key strength that the Maiden in Shadow teaches us: that it is okay to let someone else take care of you, and it is okay to need help. There are situations in life – medical, financial, even political – where it is simply not possible to fight your battles alone, or even to fight at all. The Maiden in Shadow reminds us that sometimes you really are too weak, fragile, or inexperienced to fix a situation, and that in these moments it is okay to look for a champion to take care of your interests.

THE MAIDEN IN DOMINANCE

When you manifest the Maiden in dominance, life feels like a theme park. There is so much to do, see and experience, and you want to try it all! Worries are a problem for tomorrow, and joy is the focus for today. She will lead you to live in the moment and appreciate how event the smallest of things can bring you happiness. The Maiden will remind you that life is for living, and that a positive attitude can open doors that you did not even know existed.

THE MAIDEN IN INFLUENCE

When in Influence, the Maiden tempers the nature of the other Archetypes by reminding them to believe in the best-case scenario, and to see the best in others. If the Archetype in Dominance is focussed and driven on specific goals, the Maiden is there to pull them away from their work and push them to still have a little fun with their loved ones.

THE MAIDEN IN SUBMISSION

When you push the Maiden into Submission, you have found yourself in a situation or role in life where it seems like joyous optimism has no place. It is likely that experience has taught you to expect bad outcomes or that the people around you are untrustworthy. This may well be the case, and it is worth stepping back to consider whether it is time to move on to a safer environment, or if you are suppressing the Maiden from fear of trauma.

5

THE ADVENTURER

The Adventurer is imbued with a burning desire to explore the world and find out where every road will take her. She is at her most fulfilled when she's off the beaten track, discovering new places and new customs that challenge her understanding of the world. She is a wanderer that can never stay in one place for too long, for the world is full of wonders and she wants to visit them all. The Adventurer is not naive about the potential for danger on the road, and as such believes in preparing herself in mind, body and spirit before beginning her adventures.

Even when at home, the Adventurer is always working toward her next journey. Whether that's learning a new language or saving for an upcoming trip, once she has set her sights on her next goal nothing will stop her moving toward it. Her passion can be all-consuming during this phase, and it is not unusual for her to find it difficult to talk about anything else. While she is ready and willing to see the wonder in anything new she encounters, she tends to dismiss her home as boring or unremarkable, and has very little time for her peers that choose to stay in one play for their whole lives.

The Adventurer's desire to explore the road makes it difficult for her to put down roots, and she can be hostile toward anything that ties her to a specific place for any length of time. When she is roaming, her mind can be so consumed by the moment that she forgets any obligations that have been left behind. It is not unusual for her to be out of touch for long periods of time, not because she means to be hurtful, but simply because it does not occur to her that anyone "back home" might miss her.

THE ADVENTURER IN RELATIONSHIPS

The adventurer values those people who have explored the world in their own unique way, and is never so entertained as when she's listening to the tails of travellers. She wants to be around people who are willing to push their boundaries and actively seek exposure to new cultures, and needs friends that match her desire to mix things up from time to time.

When it comes romance, the Adventurer is seeking a partner who is willing to explore the world with her rather. She is not impressed by money, status or academics, but prizes someone who is willing to grab her hand and race toward the next river, jungle, or desert. It is important to her that her travels are independent, and she expects this from her partners as well; don't expect her to buy tickets for anyone else, or to even accept someone else covering her expenses.

While the Adventurer is keen to share her journey with anyone willing to walk beside her, the call of the road will always win out over emotional ties. That isn't to say that she is heartless or uncaring, but simply that tying her down will only result in misery for all concerned. The Adventurer is a fantastic companion when out on the road, but unreliable when it comes to the usual trials of life.

THE ADVENTURER IN SHADOW

When in Shadow, the Adventurer ceases to appreciate the world she travels through, and instead begins to fetishize the cultures she explores. Her attitude can quickly turn condescending and smug, which irritates the people she comes into contact with both home and abroad.

It is surprisingly easy for the Adventurer in Shadow to remain travelling far longer than intended, especially when there are difficult times at home. She knows that running away from her problems is absolutely an option, and sees nothing wrong with ghosting people or pretending that bad things can't happen to her. So long as she is walking, she never has to look behind her at the devastation left in her wake.

At her worst, the Adventurer in Shadow has a colonial mentality in her travels, seeing the world as nothing more than a resource for her use and pleasure. She believes that the mere act of going abroad makes her a more enlightened and sophisticated individual than people who have not travelled outside their home nation, with no thought given to the barriers that they may face.

However, the Adventurer in Shadow is not purely negative. She has no time for bigotry based on race or culture, and she openly disdains those who feel superior to others for no other reason than their country of birth. She reminds us not to assume that everyone has the same experience or culture that we do, and that there is beauty to be found in all of them.

THE ADVENTURER IN DOMINANCE

When you manifest the Adventurer in Dominance, it's time to pack a bag and hit the road. It can be as low key as a visit to a nearby city, or a months-long journey backpacking through an entirely different continent, but the Adventurer needs to start moving. If that is not immediately possible, then plans need to be made and money needs to be saved, because the siren song of the world will not stop calling.

The Adventurer in Dominance provides the strength and tenacity to try something completely new, and is often a key archetype embodied by immigrants all over the world. It is no easy task to move to a new country and start life from scratch, but by manifesting her determination and powerful planning, anything can be achieved.

THE ADVENTURER IN INFLUENCE

When in Influence, the Adventurer will urge the other archetypes to look outside their own culture for answers to their problems, and reminds them that a change of scenery is often needed for the good of our souls. She will urge them to try new trails or even try blazing their own – but only if they've done their research first!

THE ADVENTURER IN SUBMISSION

When you push the Adventurer into Submission, you have given up the hope of escaping the life you are caught up in. This is not because you are happy at home, but rather because the idea of travel seems too scary, too expensive, or too daunting to attempt. While it is absolutely fine to be happy in your day to day life, remember that you don't have to go far to broaden your horizons; let the Adventurer guide you, even if it's just to a new restaurant or the next town over, because the other option is to stagnate and miss out on the wonders out in the world.

6

THE EMPRESS

The Empress is driven by a need to bring order to chaos. She believes that strong leadership is essential to bringing happiness to the maximum number of people, and is confident that she has what it takes to be the person in charge. Her focus is on building a just, fair system with clear rules that everyone can follow. Her clearly defined sense of right and wrong will not allow her to sit by when she feels the system is broken, but she will also defend those rules and laws that she feels are essential for establishing order.

The Empress is almost always found in leadership roles, whether formal or informal, as her forceful nature means others often defer to her reflexively. This is not to say she is a bully; quite the opposite in fact. The Empress truly cares for other people and wants to ensure they have what they need to thrive. Her passion for this goal is admirable, and anyone under her protection can be certain that she will fight with their best interests at heart.

As she takes her leadership responsibilities so seriously, the Empress never truly relaxes, for there is always something that needs her attention. Her quest is to stamp out chaos for the good of her people, and she is convinced that she can do it through sheer force of will. Unfortunately, this leads her to reject the truth that chaos is a fundamental part of existence, and while it is possible to tame it, chaos will never be eradicated. She does not deal well with surprises, even positive ones, because she equates order with happiness.

The desire of the Empress to bring order to the world can lead her to an obsession with bureaucracy. By designing systems that account for every eventuality rather that ones focussed on producing the desired results, she can unintentionally make life difficult and boring for the people around her. Unfortunately, her intense nature can intimidate other Archetypes, making it difficult for them to raise their concerns with her. The Empress is often surprised to learn she is perceived as unapproachable, for she knows that she will give any feedback a fair hearing, and is honest to a fault when talking with others.

THE EMPRESS IN RELATIONSHIPS

The Empress loves those she feels responsible for unconditionally, and will move heaven and earth to provide them with everything they need in life. Her affection is not always gentle, and it is always framed from what she believes others require rather than from any form of consultation. At her best, she inspires great loyalty from those around her, who will often speak of the Empress with a mixture of affection, awe, and fear.

The Empress values those people who maintain the order that she has established, and can be unforgiving toward those who break her rules in favour of Chaos. However, while she will inevitably clash with another Empress whenever they come together, she secretly admires their strength, and is proud when younger members of her circle grow fully into that power.

In romantic relationships, the Empress is often so consumed with establishing order that she gives little time or effort to finding a partner. When she does think about it, however, she tends to be attracted to people of strong moral character and a profound sense of duty to others. If she falls in love with another leader or Empress, then sparks tend to fly in a dramatic relationship. If her partner is of a quieter nature, however, the Empress will often become devoted to that person, considering their counsel indispensable, and valuing their judgement even above her own.

THE EMPRESS IN SHADOW

Of all the Archetypes, the Empress is at greatest risk of falling into Shadow. Strong leaders, especially those who have achieved great success, are often the focus of unadulterated hero-worship where their fans regard them as infallible. If the Empress is surrounded by yes-people who do not allow criticism to reach her ears, she may begin to believe she truly is beyond reproach.

The Empress in Shadow crosses the line into becoming a dictator. She uses her position and authority to enforce her will, and refuses to believe that any action she takes could be harmful. She is dismissive of the expertise of others, and will ignore any evidence that contradicts her belief that her way is the best way. At her worst, her obsession with order leads to outright hostility to anyone she regards as an agent of chaos, and she will go to extreme lengths to remove or limit their influence over her world.

In a more subtle shift, the Empress in Shadow will prize Order over the wellbeing of individual people by convincing herself that the end justifies the means. She does not care whether the people she is responsible for are happy or healthy, only that they are fulfilling the role she has assigned them to in her beautifully designed system. She conflates fairness with equality, arguing that if everyone is subject to the same rules then everyone gets the same treatment, while ignoring that some people have greater burdens and barriers in life than others.

Despite these risks, the Empress in Shadow has significant value when faced with emergency situations. She will take charge when no one else knows what to do, and quickly being establishing systems that both help people in need and restrict further harm. At moments when clear lines of leadership are necessary to get through the immediate crisis, the Empress in Shadow is not afraid to step up, get everyone organised and to make the hard decisions, even in the face of overwhelming odds. She thrives on stress and is at her best when all around her are losing their composure.

THE EMPRESS IN DOMINANCE

When you manifest the Empress in Dominance, you are taking charge of the world around you. This might manifest as being the Matriarch of your family group, or as the head of a large department in your work life. Whatever the circumstance, you need to study the mess you are attempting to clear up, and then find a clear, workable solution that protects the interests of the people you are responsible for.

The Empress in Dominance provides the strength and determination to fix what is broken, and to build up a system that ensures things do not break again. Being in a leadership position can be difficult and it can be lonely, but by manifesting the traits of the Empress in Dominance, tangible good and positive change can be achieved.

THE EMPRESS IN INFLUENCE

The Empress in influence pushes the other Archetypes to speak up and assert their authority. She will remind them that sometimes stepping onto the stage alone is the only way for your ideas to be heard, and that it is not wrong to lead the fight for positive change.

She reminds them that people are relying on them to bring about good in the world, and lends them her strength of character when they need to lead the charge.

THE EMPRESS IN SUBMISSION

With the Empress in Submission, all desire for authority or belief in self-determination is being denied. This often stems from the cultural belief that women in positions of power are "unladylike", and the societal expectation that femininity is incompatible with leadership. This is patently false.

When we place the Empress in Submission, we allow our instincts to protect and care for others to be overridden by stronger personalities. We become complicit in harmful or chaotic structures because we are unable to find the strength to fight them without the Empress there to lead us.

While there are certain circumstances where we must place the Empress in Submission for our own safety or survival, her traits are necessary for personal growth. Leadership does not always need to be out in the open; allow the Empress to lend you her determination for change.

7

THE CREATOR

The Creator is constantly brimming over with ideas for new, innovative things. She burns with the desire to bring forth something from nothing, and delights in the very act of creativity. She can be messy and chaotic or focussed and structured in her approach, but what matters most is that once she is finished, something now exists that did not exist before. Creativity exists in all aspects of our lives, and the Creator can manifest in any of them. She is responsible for the creations of new spreadsheets, new business ideas, new philosophies, and new technology. The Creator is the source of our imagination and problem-solving, for she takes her dreams and then makes them a reality.

The Creator places high value on tradition and craft, for she knows that it takes work and dedication to bring an idea into existence, but this does not make her bound by them. If the existing tools and procedures are not up to her task, then she has no qualms about trying different approaches to reach the desired result. She regards herself as an Original that was informed by what came before her, but is unique and distinct from the rest. She often manifests this aspect of herself through personal appearance and decoration of her home.

As excited by innovation in others as she is by her own work, the Creator is always interested in what her peers are producing, or what advancements are being made in other fields. She will encourage the inexperienced to commit to their craft, while cheering on the sector leaders who are pushing the creative envelope. While she is not immune to the frustration that comes with the learning process, the Creator does not let her failures and disappointments prevent her from trying to create something new, as she cannot stop creating and more than she can stop breathing.

The Creator's obsession with the production of new things can lead her to devalue that which already exists. A tendency to regard new as better can lead to wasteful habits and disdain for older work, even when it is still functional, elegant, and useful. This can make her seem pretentious or elitist at times, especially regarding material possessions.

THE CREATOR IN RELATIONSHIPS

The Creator will only tolerate being around people who accept her unique nature, and will cut ties with anyone who would force conformity upon her. While she finds many people to be boring, she values those who march to their own drum and is supportive of those exploring their identity through self expression. The Creator will always have a soft spot for the quirky members of her circle, and delights in their antics.

When in a romantic relationship, the Creator needs freedom to express her nature. Her relationships may well be of a non-traditional form but will always be governed around ideas of mutual respect. If they are to be successful, then the Creator requires that her relationships be a meeting of individuals that complement each other instead of a symbiotic whole. She needs a partner who is appreciative of her creative instincts, but that also understands her desire for the new and different.

THE CREATOR IN SHADOW

The Creator in Shadow can be exhausting for the people around her. She truly believes she is a creative genius like no other and gives no credit to the contribution of others. She is dismissive of history and heritage, seeing it as irrelevant or outdated to the creation of new things. She often takes on a large number of projects but never really completes them, and relies on hype and excitement rather than concrete results to maintain her reputation.

At her worst, the Creator in Shadow can develop something of a god complex. She is always convinced that she will be able to innovate new and better solutions to any problem, even when she has no expertise in that area. Her interference can delay or derail effective projects as she pushes for her innovations to be implemented without considering if they are appropriate or even the best.

Despite these negative traits, the Creator in Shadow can be a positive influence in the right circumstance. She is willing to champion radical ideas and out-of-the-box solutions even in the face of ridicule, and her conviction can be the source of radical improvements in many different fields. She reminds us that occasionally, our arrogant conviction in our own brilliance is based on real fact.

THE CREATOR IN DOMINANCE

With the Creator in dominance, it is almost impossible to contain all the ideas and solutions bubbling up from inside of you. There is nothing that you cannot achieve with enough imagination, and you excitedly work through and propose each idea, never losing hope that you can bring your dreams into reality. Whenever you are faced with an impossible task or a problem that feels unfixable, the

Creator in Dominance will remind you that you have both the ability and the confidence to create anything you need.

THE CREATOR IN INFLUENCE

When in Influence, the Creator brings an element of creativity to the other archetypes. By giving their strongest traits a creative twist, she enhances their strengths and allows them to come up with new ideas and approaches. Her belief in herself combined with her abundance of ideas make her a companion to any archetype looking to make a positive difference.

THE CREATOR IN SUBMISSION

When you place the Creator in Submission, you have found yourself in a role where creativity has no place, and supressing your natural urge to make improvements is necessary for survival. However, it is not healthy or wise to keep the Creator in Submission for long periods. Creation is a key trait of the Divine Feminine, and to deny it is to deny a fundamental part of who you are. Find ways to let the Creator have free rein now and again, whether that's through sketching, crafting, designing, or another method that speaks to your core being.

8

THE MOTHER

The Mother is the most nurturing of all the archetypes, and she is driven by the need to take care of others. Her focus is in helping people to recover from sickness and difficulty in their life, for she believes that all people deserve to have a kind and caring environment when they are at their weakest. She strives to make her home a welcoming and accommodating place where her guests and loved ones feel they can relax and be safe from the troubles of the world. She expresses her love through acts of service, and is always willing to go the extra mile to create a healing environment for others.

The Mother is most often found in caregiving roles, whether that is literal motherhood, healthcare, or working with the vulnerable. While she is generally considered as kind and gentle, woe betide anyone who threatens the wellbeing of her charges. She will rarely fight for her own interests, but will willingly go to war to defend those who rely on her.

Because the Mother always prioritises the needs of others over those of herself, she is at significant risk of both emotional and physical burnout. When someone needs her help, it is easy for the

Mother to be consumed with the task of providing for their needs that she forgets to take care of herself.

The Mother is so focussed with taking care of others that sometimes she forgets that they do not always need, or welcome, her protection. By obsessing over keeping them safe, she can become overbearing in her affection, to the point where she does more harm than good. The Mother is often surprised to learn that the other Archetypes can find her smothering, for she truly intends nothing more than to love and take care of those in need until they are able to take care of themselves.

THE MOTHER IN RELATIONSHIPS

The Mother is the self-appointed nurturer to all of those around her. She holds the hand of the worried, comforts the bereaved, cheers on the anxious, and shelters the scared. Her highest measure of love is defined by the services she can render, and most of her relationships are based around what help and support she can provide.

When looking for romantic partners, the Mother is drawn to the vulnerable. While she has no desire to parent a full-grown adult, her need to be needed means that she prefers people that she can help and support in their quest to be their best selves. She does not want a hopeless case but nor does she want someone who already has the answers; rather, she seeks someone who will appreciate her skills without taking advantage of her nature.

THE MOTHER IN SHADOW

When in Shadow, the Mother crosses the line from nurturing and supportive into domineering and controlling. She is so convinced that she knows what is best for the people she is caring for, that she overrides their opinions in favour of her own preferences. The Mother in Shadow tends to infantilize others, especially if they were once dependent on her for their care, and it seems like she regards everyone else as children, and herself as the only adult in the room.

At her worst, the Mother in Shadow will find ways to make and keep others dependent on her, as her entire identity becomes caught up in the idea of herself as a saint or martyr. She encourages learned helplessness and reliance on her aid in the people around her, and will then use her sacrifices as a way to manipulate and guilt them into staying in her influence. While she is not as strong as other archetypes in Shadow, it is arguable that the Mother in Shadow can do the most harm on an individual level, for what she presents as unconditional love and willing sacrifice can be weaponized to shame those in her care.

The positive nature of the Mother in Shadow is to remind us that while it is noble to provide help and nurture to others, it is often acceptable to expect acknowledgement, or even gratitude, if we go significantly out of our way to provide care. That is not to say a parade should be thrown for every act of basic human decency, but rather to be aware that some people will try to take advantage of our kindness, or have unreasonable expectations on our heart and our time.

THE MOTHER IN DOMINANCE

When you manifest the Mother in Dominance, you are taking bringing the vulnerable in your circle under your wing. This might manifest as being the primary caregiver to a family member in need, or as a mentoring relationship with a new entrant into your chosen field. The Mother in Dominance remind you that everyone can be weak or vulnerable depending on the circumstances of their life, and that it is a noble act to help them recover their strength.

The Mother in Dominance is an acknowledgement that bad things can happen to anyone, even good people, and that even the strongest person can be knocked down unexpectedly. She embodies compassion and empathy when dealing with the people around her, for we are all one bad day away from finding ourselves reliant on others.

THE MOTHER IN INFLUENCE

When in Influence, the Mother encourages a softer, more intuitive approach when dealing with the people around us. She encourages the other archetypes to consider the reasons why opposing parties might be hostile to suggestions, or to remember the potential for human suffering that their action or inaction might cause. The Mother in Influence reminds us that people are more than just numbers, and that we have an obligation to care for those in need.

THE MOTHER IN SUBMISSION

The Mother in Submission involves the removal of empathy when dealing with other people. Without her influence, it is easy to focus on the "big picture" without considering the human cost of actions. While this is sometimes necessary, especially when hard decisions need to be made, the Mother is essential for us to effectively channel the Feminine Divine in a meaningful way. If you have found yourself placing the Mother in Submission on a regular basis, it is time to examine why you are hostile to the idea that other people are worthy of compassion and love.

THE PRIESTESS

The Priestess is the holder of secret knowledge, of intuition and of dreams. She represents the power of the subconscious and our ability to pick up on subtext. Her powers can seem otherworldly when she accurately predicts the future, and friends will seek her out for her guidance on complex matters. The Priestess understands how people work and the rhythms of the natural world so deeply that they have become a kind of sixth sense, and she relies on this to help her navigate through life. If her instinct is screaming at her that a scenario is wrong or dangerous, she will trust it and act accordingly, even if logic and reason tells her otherwise.

The Priestess believes that we are all able to access such powers, but that the modern world has both corrupted and disrupted their use. She understands that it takes time and study to develop these skills, and frets that society denies many the tools they need to work on them; namely, quiet space and the natural environment.

It is not unusual for the Priestess to be involved in some esoteric practices as a way to focus and guide her intuition, although her tools of choice will vary greatly depending on her cultural background. These practices or artefacts are usually seen as a focus or touchstone for her beliefs about her abilities rather than as magical objects that grant power to anyone that touches them. Whatever she believes to be the source or reason behind her intuitive capabilities, the Priestess understands that they are not unique to her, and that with the right training and environment, they can be developed by anyone.

The Priestess is also the embodiment of transformation. Like the alchemists of old who sought to turn base metal into gold, the Priestess is on a journey to make both herself and the world around her into better versions. Her goal is harmonious balance, where people are connected to and responsible for the environment around them. She believes that many of society's ills are caused by a disconnect from nature and the resulting imbalance in our lives.

Sometimes the Priestess forgets that her intuitive understanding of the world can mistaken for religious fervor or supernatural powers by those from a different tradition. This can lead her to be dismissed as a charlatan or extremist, and damage the very causes that she is trying to champion. She can find it frustrating when people demand how she knows the things that she knows, but then will not accept her explanations of how she believes the process works. It can be challenging for the Priestess to bridge the gap between the esoteric and the mundane worlds, but if anyone can find a way to make that connection, it is her.

The Priestess in relationships

The Priestess is governed by her intuitive judgement of people, and will modify her behaviour towards them based on that intuition. She values her gut feelings over actions or words, because she knows that humans are complicated and can hide their true nature. If she truly dislikes someone then she tends to be unfailingly polite rather than hostile, for she knows that setting up acrimonious relationships can be disruptive to their social environment. The Priestess prefers to be around people that love and respect the natural world, and who strive to leave the world a better place than they found it.

When it comes to romance, the Priestess believes in soul mates, love at first sight, and the balance of the Feminine and Masculine Divine. Her love in engaged deeply, and her partner will become an essential part of her happiness. She will usually fall for people with either people whose outlook on life is similar to her own, or someone who is passionate about their work in nature or the environment.

The Priestess is sensitive to changes in mood and expects her partner to be the same, which can lead to breakdowns in communication and unrealistic expectations. Once she has decided that she loves someone, however, the Priestess will be unfailingly loyal and attentive, even in the face of betrayal, for she cannot bear the thought that her intuition might have been wrong.

THE PRIESTESS IN SHADOW

The Priestess in Shadow can be a dangerous and destructive figure. She believes her intuition is not the result of study and experience, but is a gift from the Divine that makes her special and superior to those without it. She begins to conflate her desires with the intuitive process, and at her worst can act like any thought she has is sacrosanct.

The Priestess in Shadow uses her understanding of human nature to control and manipulate those who look up to her, seeking to make them reliant on her for guidance and advice. She will use pageantry and props to give herself an air of the supernatural, although it is not always clear if she believes in her power to use these tools, or is behaving as a charlatan.

Although the Priestess in Shadow can use her powers for good, her path is a difficult one to walk. She can use her influence over others to inspire them to make the world better, but her intentions can be corrupted quickly and without her awareness. If you choose to manifest the Priestess in Shadow, tread carefully, for she can cause untold damage to others all in the name of Light.

THE PRIESTESS IN DOMINANCE

When you manifest the Priestess in Dominance, you are in tune with the rhythms of the world and people around you, and sensitive to the slightest shift in balance. Your intuition will act as the conduit between your subconscious knowledge and your making mind, allowing you to gain additional insight and understanding. You navigate life with your feelings rather than intellect, with the goal of creating harmony and balance all around you.

The Priestess in Dominance will guide you to learn about mysticism, religion, and arcane practices, not to gain power over others, but as tools to help you develop your intuition and understanding. You will reject many and be drawn to others, but be sure to remember that they are merely processes of learning about the natural world, and not weapons that you should wield for personal gain.

THE PRIESTESS IN INFLUENCE

When in Influence, the Priestess reminds the other Archetypes to check in with their gut reactions when faced with tasks or challenges. She does not denigrate the roles of logic and data, but rather sees them as complemented by intuition and feeling.

The Priestess in Influence also provides context to the decision making process by pointing out that since we cannot help but review information and data through our own cultural viewpoint, then it is better to explicitly recognise and use our intuition instead of denying its existence.

THE PRIESTESS IN SUBMISSION

The most common reason people have for placing the Priestess in Submission is that their intuition is in direct conflict with their desire. It could be that they wish for a relationship with a specific individual, but that something in their subconscious is warning them that it is a mistake because it has picked up on subtle red flags that the conscious mind has missed. If their desire for the relationship is too strong, then they will suppress the Priestess and her intuition so that they can pursue that individual.

If you are choosing to place the Priestess in Submission, then ask yourself why you feel it is necessary to ignore your gut feelings, and what you need to do to learn how to trust them again.

10

THE HUNTER

*T*he Hunter is the ultimate provider. While she is capable of surviving and even thriving on her own, she knows that humans function best when part of a society, and uses her skills to help and support those around her. Her greatest joy comes from protecting those who cannot defend themselves, and she is not afraid to get dirty in the process.

The Hunter understands that the world is not perfect, and that there are all manner of threats hiding in the shadows. If someone in her community is hurt, then she will hunt down the threat and neutralize it. If her community needs food, shelter, or other needs, then she will track down the resources and bring them home for her people. If someone is in danger, then she's the first person on the scene to make sure they get home safely.

Preferring action to discussion, the Hunter takes a very pragmatic view to life, and tends to react to the situation at hand rather than worrying about what might be. This is not the same as being reckless with resources; she knows a surplus of food is better than a shortage, and that preventing a flood is better than cleaning up after one. She is in touch with the rhythms of her environment, and seeks to maintain the balance necessary for her community to thrive.

The Hunter has little interest in the world beyond her immediate environment, or in the people outside of her sphere of responsibility. She is not concerned about philosophical issues, politics, or what people she doesn't know are doing with their lives, so long as they are not causing problems for community. Her attitude is to live and let live, but if you hurt her family then she will seek out and destroy you. The Hunter has no need or interest in wealth accumulation or gaining status in the community, or much time for those that do, but she does believe that comfort and security are deserved by all, and that those who can take care of others, like herself, have an obligation to do so.

THE HUNTER IN RELATIONSHIPS

If you are loved by the Hunter they may never actually say the words, but you know it without question because of their actions. If you are hurt they won't waste time trying to console you, but will set about fixing you up before you know what is happening. The Hunter will do anything and sacrifice her own needs to make sure there is a roof over your head and food in your stomach, but will be surprised, or even offended, if you try to thank her for it. Her love is demonstrated through acts of service, and there is nothing she would not do for those she loves. She can be surprisingly gentle and patient with people in crisis, but will not suffer fools or those who try to take advantage of her skills. For anyone in any kind of trouble, the Hunter is the person they trust to have their back.

The Hunter takes a pragmatic approach to love compared to the other archetypes, and is only happy with a partner who accepts that to love her means loving her whole clan. She will never shirk her responsibilities, even if it costs her all-personal happiness, because her priority will always be to provide for her people. A partner that both understands and celebrates this about the Hunter is essential for making a romantic relationship work.

THE HUNTER IN SHADOW

When in Shadow, the Hunter becomes a predator. She will use the excuse of being a provider to excuse behaviours that go beyond the need of taking care of those she loves. She ceases to care about balance in favour of hoarding resources for her own family, claiming that their need is superior to those of other groups.

The Hunter in Shadow will see anyone outside of her group as suspicious, or even an enemy, to the wellbeing of her community. She will seek to remove these perceived threats by any means necessary, and is not above lying, stealing, or even violence to reach her goals. Rather than believing in balance, she sees the world as a competition where there is not enough to go around.

However, the Hunter in Shadow can have a positive impact in our lives. When hard decisions need to be made, particularly those with no good outcomes, the Hunter in Shadow can step where others would be paralysed. She also understands that there are, on rare occasions, times when causing short term or limited harm is necessary to prevent a greater tragedy. She might not be very nice when in this role, but the Hunter in Shadow can perform distasteful tasks that are in line with her integrity while fully aware that she may be cast a villain for her act. She reminds us that sometimes there is nothing you can do to stop something bad from happening, but if you have the courage to act, you can at least reduce the severity.

THE HUNTER IN DOMINANCE

When you manifest the Hunter in Dominance, you feel that you are responsible for meeting the needs of those you care for. It could be that you work long hours to provide financial support for your family, or are a community advocate for a vulnerable demographic. Whatever the role, you are driven by a need to make sure that basic needs are met, and are only happy when those you are about are safe.

The Hunter in Dominance lends her patience and cool head to anyone facing a threat to their community's basic wellbeing, for she is relentless in seeking out resources and will not stop until she takes care of their needs. If you ever feel like giving up in the face of impossible odds, the Hunter in Dominance will help you keep on striving for a solution – so long as your goal is fuelled by necessity and not greed.

THE HUNTER IN INFLUENCE

The Hunter in Influence is vocal in her dislike of materialism and greed, so will constantly question the other archetypes as to why they are pursuing certain goals. She will urge them to consider whether their actions will result in security, comfort and balance, or whether they will disturb the natural harmony of their environment for personal gain. In crisis situations or times of real distress, the Hunter in Influence pushes the other Archetypes to remember that others are also suffering, and not to forget that humans need to work as a community if they are to thrive.

THE HUNTER IN SUBMISSION

When you push the Hunter into Submission, you are forsaking all responsibility for the wellbeing or others. This is not just prioritising your personal needs so that you can stay strong, but a deliberate act of removing empathy for others so that you do not have to think about the impact of your actions.

People who keep the Hunter in Submission for prolonged periods will often try to take the title of "lone wolf" as a badge of honour, but do not be fooled as there is nothing honourable about greed or lack of empathy. If you are guilty of forcing the Hunter into Submission, it is time to re-evaluate your approach to other people and start listening to the Hunter's guidance.

11

THE REBEL

The Rebel is the misfit of the Archetypes, the revolutionary and iconoclast who sees the rules of society more like guidelines rather than laws. She is driven by a desire to make the world a better place and has no concerns putting herself on the front line to protect those who cannot protect themselves. She actively distrusts anyone with a vested interest in maintaining authority over others, and openly advocates for anyone in power to be held to a higher standard of behaviour than the general public.

The Rebel is the embodiment of the need to escape the constraints of a mundane life and to set our own rules. She is not an anarchist, however, as it's not that she objects to the existence of law; it's more that she only follows the ones she believes in. She respects expertise in others when it is earned, but that doesn't mean she will always agree with their way of doing things. She has no issue with using shock value or outrageous behaviours to disrupt activities she takes issue with or shake people out of their perceived complacency.

Though the Rebel is romanticized by society for her strong moral compass, in reality her methods too often stray into questionable territory. The Rebel is not here for slow change or incremental improvements, preferring to tear everything down first and figure out how to fix it later. She is not only willing but enthusiastic about breaking the law, leading to actions that are damaging or even outright dangerous. It is not uncommon for her to alienate the very people she needs to win over, which only feeds her sense of it being her against the world.

It is important to remember that simply rebelling against a rule or system is not the same as truly manifesting the Rebel; she does not revel in shock value for its own sake, but to make the point that the status quo needs to change. To put it simply, wearing black and joining a rock band is not an act of the Rebel, but wearing black and joining a rock band as a way to protest government censorship is.

Despite the controversy she may draw by her actions, the Rebel is responsible for great change in the world. She is not afraid to stand up for the powerless, is not afraid to draw fire in her direction, and will never turn a blind eye to suffering. At her best she is capable of great acts than can change the course of history toward a better future, even if her methods are not always orthodox. The truth is that the Rebel can make us uncomfortable when we deserve to be uncomfortable, and her fearless nature deserves to be celebrated.

THE REBEL IN RELATIONSHIPS

The Rebel is always willing and ready to fight for the people she loves – even if they are the ones begging her not to get involved. She will never let an injustice stand, and there is no length she won't go to for the people that she loves.

Unfortunately, her love for her family and friends involves pushing them out of their own comfort zones and confronting anything that the Rebel feels should be opposed. Her activism may be well intentioned, but it can be exhausting and unending – especially if her loved ones have a different opinion.

When it comes to romantic relationships, the Rebel is unique among the Archetypes in that she is only really attracted to other Rebels. Her dedication to fighting the power leaves no room for people complicit to the system she wants to tear down, so unless a potential partner is committed to the same cause as the Rebel, their relationship is doomed to fail. Even then, she will always be willing to sacrifice for the Cause, whatever that might be, and that includes friends, relationships, and even her lovers.

THE REBEL IN SHADOW

The Rebel in Shadow is no longer motivated by a need to better the world, but a need to enact change at any cost. Though her ultimate goal might still be a noble one, the Rebel in Shadow has lost all sense of perspective, with dangerous acts of vandalism or even terror never removed from the table.

The Rebel in Shadow is dogmatic about her chosen cause, refusing to listen to other perspectives about how change can be enacted. She will cast out anyone who does not fit her narrow definition of "right" or "good" and will recategorize former allies as enemies if she feels they have somehow sold out on there beliefs. If the people she is fighting for believe she is doing them more harm than good, she will dismiss their concerns as the result of weakness, cowardice, or lack of education, never stopping to consider that she might be wrong. The rebel sees no room for forgiveness, and if you are not in perfect agreement with her beliefs about the world, then you become disposable in her eyes.

At her worst, the Rebel in Shadow is willing to commit crimes and cause significant harm to innocent parties so long as she feels that her point has been made to authority. She has lost her morality and finds herself alienated from her loved ones, until the only people at her side are fellow extremists. Even the cause gets replaced with a hatred of authority and a need for vengeance at any cost, making the Rebel in Shadow a dangerous archetype to manifest.

At her best, however, the Rebel in Shadow is the embodiment of fighting against impossible odds in the name of doing the right thing. She is the manager who sacrifices her job by standing up for the workers, even though she knows that her being fired has not changed anything. She is the soldier who holds her position even when defeat and death are inevitable, not because she believes it will make a difference to the war, but because it was important that she at least *try*. The same unyielding nature that can make her a villain can also make her a martyr, although whatever option she chooses, the Rebel in Shadow never walks an easy path.

THE REBEL IN DOMINANCE

When you manifest the Mother in Dominance, you are taking bringing the vulnerable in your circle under your wing. This might manifest as being the primary caregiver to a family member in need, or as a mentoring relationship with a new entrant into your chosen field. The Mother in Dominance remind you that everyone can be weak or vulnerable depending on the circumstances of their life, and that it is a noble act to help them recover their strength.

The Mother in Dominance is an acknowledgement that bad things can happen to anyone, even good people, and that even the strongest person can be knocked down unexpectedly. She embodies compassion and empathy when dealing with the people around her, for we are all one bad day away from finding ourselves reliant on others.

THE REBEL IN INFLUENCE

When in Influence, the Rebel screams from the sidelines that it's time for less talk and more action. She reminds the other archetypes that it is okay to be unpopular and it is okay to make people uncomfortable so long as you believe in the morality of your cause.

The Rebel in Influence will bring creative suggestions to the table and point out that public awareness of problems and wrongdoing are the key to bringing about change. She makes the other Archetypes uncomfortable by challenging them about their participation in the system that has brought about the situation they find themselves in, and always gets them to ask, "who benefits from the status quo?"

THE REBEL IN SUBMISSION

With the Rebel in Submission, you are turning a blind eye to the problems of the world around you, no matter their size. Of all the archetypes, the Rebel is the one we most commonly force into submission, for while we may love her aesthetic, it is uncomfortable to examine all the ways we are complicit in harming others and damaging the world around us. To paraphrase Abolitionist campaigner William Wilberforce, *you can choose to look away but you can never again pretend that you did not know*. With the Rebel in Submission, it is easier to ignore the harm and maintain the status quo than it is to admit wrongdoing and make the necessary changes. If you are guilty of keeping the Rebel in Submission, it's time to let her out, and to let her talk.

12

THE LOVER

The Lover desires human connection and sensual pleasure above all things. Passion drives her forward, for the Lover never does anything by half measure. She wants the best of everything; the best clothes, because of how they feel on her skin; the best food for the way it stimulates her taste buds, and the best art for the visual indulgence it provides for her. More than anything, however, the Lover desires people around her to share in these experiences and whose admiration for beautiful things matches or exceeds her own.

Because she is concerned about her appearance and of looking her best at all times, the Lover is often dismissed as a shallow or vain creature, when in truth this archetype is more complicated than that. She experiences the world on a sensual level, and so believes that the best way to live life is to indulge those senses with the best things available. As she presumes that many, if not most people share her approach to existence, she believes that the only way to attract the interest of the best people in the world is for her to be the living embodiment of the best sensual experience.

As a result, the Lover is usually a talented individual with an exceptional appreciation of art, music, culture, and food. When at her best, the Lover has no desire to keep these pleasures locked away for an elite few to enjoy, but rather seeks to bring them to as many people as possible. The Lover is not ignorant of the ugly side of the world, but her way of combatting such woes is through making pleasurable experiences easier to access.

The Lover will often draw criticism for her reliance on sexual and sensual appeal as a tool for achieving her goal. She is always happy to indulge in light flirtation, and sees no reason for denying herself the pleasure of physical intimacy so long as it is both desired and consensual on all sides. As she is in tune with the sensual desires of others, she sees sex as no different than gifting fine wine, Belgian truffles, designer clothing, or a private music performance when in pursuit of a particular outcome. The key, however, always comes down to pleasure, for she enjoys the act of giving. The moment the Lover feels that such gifts are expected or demanded by others, she will end such interactions. The Lover staunchly believes that only things given or received freely and without strings are true sources of pleasure, and is the first to condemn anyone who would expect such things as their due.

THE LOVER IN RELATIONSHIPS

The Lover will be there for every important moment in the lives of those she adores, usually bearing flowers, chocolates, or wine most suited to the occasion. She will laugh, cry, and commiserate at their side when emotions are running high, but she's not always around for things that are mundane or boring. After all, the Lover craves sensual experience of any type, so while she will be there to hold someone's hand at a funeral, she's nowhere to be found if someone needs a ride to the hardware store.

In romantic relationships, the Lover expects to be courted and wooed in as indulgent a manner as possible. This does not mean everything has to be expensive or designer, but rather that each experience must be a quality one. She seeks a partner who is attractive, educated, cultured and sophisticated, and spends a great deal of her own resources in matching that ideal within herself. Physical attraction is important to the Lover, as is sexual compatibility, as her need for sensual experience means that her partner's preferences and skills must match her own.

On the surface it is easy to dismiss the Lover's relationship preferences as shallow, but it must be remembered that her desire to experience the best of everything means that once she's found her partner, she will be both loyal and devoted to them. After all, she knows that her partner is the best person out there, whatever others might believe, and she can happily spend the rest of her days with her chosen mate exploring the finer things in life.

The Lover also represents our need for, and understanding of, the power of human connection. The Lover expresses her affection through touch, whether that's with a quick hug, a firm handshake, a platonic kiss, or a passionate embrace. The Lover is there for people at the best of times and the worst of times, for what is life for if not being there to experience the full range of human emotion?

THE LOVER IN SHADOW

When in Shadow, the Lover's need for human connection and pleasure switches to dependency and over-indulgence. She forgets that pleasure is not the same as joy, and relies on sensory stimulation as a mask to cover her unhappiness. Rather than trying to fix the underlying problems in her life, the Lover will surround herself with luxurious items and increasingly hedonistic pleasures, until financial woes and addictions become too large to ignore.

The Lover in Shadow is terrified of being alone. Instead of allowing the relationships and friendships in her life take a natural course, she can become demanding of time and attention from others, and deeply jealous whenever she is not the centre of attention. Her neediness can become toxic and controlling if left unchecked, until she drives away the very people who she wanted to love her.

At her worst, the Lover in Shadow will use her sensuality to ensnare and manipulate other people codependent relationships, even when they fall far short of her ideal, because her biggest fear is being alone and deprived of that human connection. She will provide possessions and indulgences, including illicit substances, to people she knows are using her in exchange for the appearance of friendship and affection. The Lover will ignore the harm and devastation such behaviour will leave in its wake in favour of her charade, for the threat of being abandoned and forgotten is worse than any other consequences from her actions.

THE LOVER IN DOMINANCE

When you manifest the Lover in Dominance, it is time to embrace your inner diva and splash out on whatever luxuries you can afford. The Lover knows you are worthy of the best, and sees no reason accept substandard experiences when you do not have to. With the Lover in Dominance, reach out to your circle and find ways to share their passions and pleasures together, for nothing will build relationships faster than connecting over a mutual love.

Even when facing an overwhelmingly dark experience, the Lover in Dominance can guide you through the day. She values touch, and knows that sometimes what people need the most is not money, supplies or even an advocate; what they need is someone to hold their hand when they are scared, or to hug them while they cry. When everything feels hopeless and like there are no actions that can be taken to improve the situation, manifesting the Lover in Dominance will give you empathy and strength necessary just be physically present for someone that needs you. Through her power, you will see that what people need the most is human connection. What they need, is you.

THE LOVER IN INFLUENCE

When in Influence, the Lover advocates for adding a little sensuality into your life. She understands that people are far more likely to do things they find enjoyable that things that are distasteful, or even just dull, so why not try to make things that much more pleasurable for all? Even if there is no way to distract from or reduce the darker side of work that needs to be done, the Lover is here to remind the other archetypes that providing a reward or a small slice of pleasure on an otherwise terrible day can help people through the hardest moments of their lives.

THE LOVER IN SUBMISSION

When you push the Lover into Submission, the need for human connection does not disappear, but is simply being ignored. While abstinence from specific substances or experiences may be necessary for your health or happiness, abstaining from all pleasures in life is not conducive to a positive existence. When the Lover is in Submission, it is common for the missing pleasures to be replaced by other sensory experiences that are unhealthy or harmful, until the need to feel or cause pain is indistinguishable from the desire for happiness and pleasure. Remember that pleasure comes from the beautiful things in the world that belong to the Light; instead of shunning them completely by placing the Lover in Submission, instead remind yourself that moderation is a more achievable, and sustainable, goal to have.

13

THE FAE

The Fae is the trickster and comedian of the Divine Feminine Archetypes, who has seen the absurdity and chaos of existence, and decided to laugh at it. She's perfectly aware that the world can be a cruel and unjust place, but instead of getting upset or angry, she uses mockery and frivolity as her weapons of choice. Don't be fooled by her happy-go-lucky attitude to the world; the Fae is intelligent, cunning, and far more tricksy that anyone realises.

The Fae believes that laughter is good for the soul, and it is her mission in life to bring cheer and humour to the world. She finds it difficult to be around the more thoughtful and earnest Archetypes for prolonged periods, especially those in positions of power, because they rarely laugh at themselves or see the ridiculous in serious situations. The Fae sees this as evidence of self-importance and pomposity, and feels it is her sacred duty to bring them down a peg or two.

Her determination to laugh in the face of every challenge or absurdity can make the Fae difficult to deal with. While everyone finds her an amusing companion at least some of the time, many are offended when she laughs at incidents they feel should make her cry. The Fae's dark humour is a coping strategy and a choice to prevent her being crushed by the Shadow aspect of society, but it is often misunderstood as a cruel or selfish reaction.

The Fae, however, never punches down. She never laughs at those who are vulnerable or oppressed, although she may laugh at the ridiculousness of the situation. She believes that anyone in power or authority should expect to be mocked by those without influence, and is more than willing to lead the charge on this point.

Loved by many, loathed by many, loved and loathed together by those who know her the best, the Fae is both a blessing and a curse to those around her, but they would not have her any other way.

THE FAE IN RELATIONSHIPS

The Fae is usually the Funny One in any social or family group, although her style can range from class clown to sarcasm queen. While she is careful not to use her wit to bully or victimize people with less power than she holds herself, she can be merciless when teasing her peers. She delights in light-hearted tricks or pranks, for although people might be on the receiving end of her jokes at times, they are never meant or delivered in a frame of mockery or contempt.

Having said that, big family gathering are fraught with danger if both the Fae and your racist old uncle are in the same room. No one will be quite sure how far the Fae will push the line of her mockery, or whether your uncle will even pick up on her jokes in the first place. Remember, however, that animosity toward the Fae is usually misplaced; if your uncle had not felt safe enough to tell his bigoted anecdotes in the first pace, then she would never have aimed her knife-sharp humour at his kneecaps.

A romantic relationship with the Fae will be a lot of things, but boring is not one of them. She will play pranks, set up elaborate tricks, or just make her partner burst out laughing at inappropriate moments all in the name of happiness. Her partners will alternate between laughing with her and groaning in despair at her latest antics, but they know she only teases her equals, and saves her most outlandish pranks for the person she loves the most.

THE FAE IN SHADOW

The Fae in Shadow no longer wields her humour for the entertainment of others, but as a vindictive and cruel weapon. She takes out her frustrations with the state of the world on those least responsible for them, punching down to regain a false sense of power and control. Her jokes cut deep, and she targets them to places designed to cause the maximum amount of pain to the recipient.

The Fae in Shadow hides her darkness behind the immortal and inaccurate words: *it was just a joke*. She does not like to be called out on her cruelty because it runs counter to her self-image as joker who uses humour to speak Truth to Power, so she turns the tables on her victims whenever possible, making it seem like their inability to laugh at her bullying makes them the real bullies, and herself but an innocent victim.

The Fae in Shadow, when channeled for good, uses her quick wit and cutting humour to make society face the darkest parts of our nature and society, and ask ourselves why we allowed these situations to come about. Her pranks call attention to injustice rather than exploiting it, and while she may make certain people or institutions into objects of ridicule with her antics, it is only to shine a light on the harm that they are responsible for. This is a delicate weapon to wield, however, and should only be done by the most skilled of comedians.

THE FAE IN DOMINANCE

When you manifest the Fae in Dominance laughter swirls all around you. You know that humour is a remarkably effective tool with a wide variety of uses, and delight in your ability to make life that little bit better for the people around you, even if it's only for a short while.

The Fae in Dominance will teach you that it is okay to play the fool sometimes, and that constantly being serious doesn't make you a better person. She gives you the courage to laugh at the things that scare you, and the insight to wield your wit as a tool to undermine the bullies and despots of your life.

Most of all, though, the Fae in Dominance connects you to others through laughter. She knows that comedy, when done with integrity and positive intent, builds bridges and opens doors, allowing communication and camaraderie between the most surprising of pairings. The Fae in Dominance will make you grin at your enemies; it will make them start to worry what prank you've set up at their expense, and make them regret that they every tried to mess with you.

THE FAE IN INFLUENCE

When in Influence, the Fae rolls her eyes at the other Archetypes and tells them to try laughing once in a while. Her role is to remind the others that being dour and relentlessly serious will give them an ulcer, so it's time to see the funny side of things. When facing off against a powerful opponent, the Fae will cheerfully suggest blowing raspberries at them or throwing a nonsensical insult in their direction, not to cause offense, but to make them appear ridiculous. The Fae understands that humour can be a subtle tool in any arsenal, and is ready to hand over the whoopee cushions and glitter bombs to her sisters.

THE FAE IN SUBMISSION

People who prize solemnity as the outward display of intelligence often place the Fae in Submission, depriving themselves of the ability to see the funny side of things. By mistaking a serious demeanour with proof of integrity, they will sometimes take a perverse pleasure in finding comedy to be beneath their notice. The Fae is not just about pranks and slapstick; she calls the powerful to account, challenges unfair power dynamics, and provides courage in the face of failure by helping us to see how silly things can be, or by giving us a brief moment of happiness to see us through the bad times. Let the Fae out of Submission, and try to follow her lead, for it is only in the darkness that light can truly shine.

14

THE FRIEND

The Friend is the most ordinary of all the Archetypes, and embodies the desire to live a good life. She is gloriously average in all things, and are motivated by a sense of community, belonging, and simple pleasures. The Friend just wants everyone to get along. She believes that everyone should try their best to contribute to building their community, but also that the community should be there for those in need. If things are generally more good than bad for those around her, then she prefers to maintain the status quo than chase any hypothetical improvements. After all, if it isn't broken, then there's no point in trying to fix it.

At her best when surrounded by people, the Friend will be the first to champion any group initiative that brings a community together, whether that's through social gatherings, barn raisings, litter picks or food drives. Even if she is the one who organises the event, don't try to single her out for special attention; she resents anyone being put on a pedestal, even herself, and honestly believes that someone else would have stepped into the role if she had been unavailable.

The Friend values the simple pleasures in life, like a meal with a friend or a homemade sweater. She wants to share her comforts with her peers, but resents anyone who tries to make themselves appear better than the rest of the community. She actively distrusts authority figures or anyone considered to be of higher social status, not because she is jealous, but because she believes that power is a corrupting influence and that the Elite only gained their position by stepping on the backs of others.

The Friend has no time for what she considers pretension; she is proud of her genuine nature and that what you see is what you get with her. You can trust her to keep her word and turn up when she says that she will, because maintaining the unwritten social contract is a core part of her philosophy, and while she may never openly criticize those who are unreliable, she is silently judging them for not turning up when they are needed.

It is easy to stereotype or laugh at the Friend, because she is not exciting, opinionated or motivated to make her mark upon history. Her life can seem small and unimportant to the more driven Archetypes, but in truth, the Friend is the glue that holds the world together, and is responsible for more happiness and stability in her social circle than any genius or hero has managed to achieve. Without the Friend in the background making sure everything runs smoothly, society would have fallen apart a long time ago.

THE FRIEND IN RELATIONSHIPS

The Friend will be there for people before they ask, and genuinely cares for the wellbeing of those around her – even those she doesn't particularly like. She is adept at organising others whether they wanted to help or not, and yet somehow leaves everyone feeling content and glad that they participated. She is the subject of good-natured teasing from those in her community, but they appreciate all she does and they know how much they need her, for she is the heart of every group, family and circle she belongs to.

In romantic relationships, the Friend seeks a partner that is loving, empathetic, and hardworking, but also someone that understands they will always have to share her with the community. Her drive to be a good neighbour will never diminish, and so an ideal mate would be someone who is willing to be at her side for any community endeavour, and comfortable dressing up while they are at it.

Because the Friend will give of herself without question, it is important that she has a partner and friends who know when to intercede and force her to rest. She is at constant risk of being taken advantage of by others which inevitably leads to burnout, and so she relies on other Archetypes to protect her from her own nature at times.

THE FRIEND IN SHADOW

When in Shadow, the Friend ceases to be part of the community out of love, and instead participates from a fear of being abandoned. Her greatest fear is being left to face the hardships of life without her support network, and so she will do anything to maintain the status quo in her circle.

At her worst, the Friend in Shadow becomes exclusionary and fearful towards anything she deems a threat or upset to her ordered little world. This thinking can lead to bigotry, where instead of welcoming and including others into her community, she either rejects them completely, or attempts to "fix" the things that make the person different.

The Friend in Shadow will also bury any concerns or opinions she might have about the direction her community is going in and choose to conform to the societal norms, even when they trouble her conscience. She will say yes to things she does not want to do or turn a blind eye to the suffering of others so long as most of her group remains happy. If left unchecked, the Friend in Shadow will lose her sense of personal identity in favour of the mask she has chosen to wear, until the mask is all she has left.

THE FRIEND IN DOMINANCE

When you manifest the Friend in Dominance, you are choosing a simple life that is focussed on building a strong, connected community. You are an excellent team player who will put her energy into creating and maintaining strong bonds of mutual appreciation, because you know that an effective team will always have better results than the lone-wolf genius.

The Friend in Dominance will release your sociable side, and gift you with respect for the hard-working nature of the common person. She will show you the true beauty and value of simple acts of kindness, reminding you that even the smallest amount of good that you do in the world still adds up to a better world.

THE FRIEND IN INFLUENCE

When in Influence, the Friend will question the other Archetypes about how their actions effect the ordinary masses. She will loudly remind them that "acceptable losses" or "the ends justifying the means" impacts and hurts real world people, and forces them to confront the consequences of their decisions, intentional or otherwise. The Friend in Influence pushes the other Archetypes to take a look behind the curtain before they make any decisions, and to always ask who stands to benefit from any action that can hurt the members of the community.

THE FRIEND IN SUBMISSION

When you push the Friend into Submission, you have chosen to believe that not everyone has equal worth or value. You have abandoned the social contract that demands you take care of those less fortunate than yourself, and embraced the belief that the upper classes and social elites are there because they truly are superior to other people.

Placing the Friend in Submission allows you to ignore the complex reality of real life and to ignore your obligations to take care of others. It allows you to buy into the myth of self-made success so that you can remove any guilt for not trying to make life better for the majority instead of just yourself.

While it can sometimes be necessary to put the Friend in Submission so you can escape toxic communities and high-control groups, do not leave her there for long; it is the Friend that will help you to build a new social network, and we all need people we can rely on in the tough times.

15

NEXT STEPS

*O*nce you are familiar with the Archetypes and have considered the ways to integrate them into your conscious self, it is time to study the interplay between them and the Divine Feminine traits discussed earlier in this book. Journal and meditate on how each Archetype embodies or rejects each trait in both light and shadow. Pay attention to the combinations that resonate with you, and those that you find distasteful. It is only through understanding your reactions to them that you will learn to embrace and celebrate the Divine Feminine within your core self.

As part of your study, take the time to learn about and study how other cultures treat the concept of the Divine Feminine, and where their beliefs intersect with the role of women in their societies. Use both ancient and existing civilisations for this work, and be prepared to dig deeply into the literature to learn the nuance and often contradictory beliefs about what constitutes Feminine and Masculine in any given culture, and apply your understanding of the Archetypes against these beliefs. You will find that what one society considers as the embodiment of the Feminine Divine is classed as Sacred Masculine in another, while the tasks associated with genders will also differ greatly. Approach this study with the wonder of the Maiden and the logic of the Scholar; remember that the Masculine and Feminine energies are not separate but part of an integrated whole that flows and swirls, making room for more than one iteration of balance.

Remember that this is not a process that you will ever truly complete; the more you learn about the interplay between the Divine Feminine and the Divine Masculine, and the more you learn about the balance between Light and Shadow, you will always discover something new to study about yourself and others. There will always be new experiences and new perspectives for you to explore, and the lack of a final destination on this journey is something that should be celebrated.

16

RECONCILING WITH THE SACRED MASCULINE

When first embarking on a journey to embrace the Divine Feminine, it is not uncommon for people to question their relationship with the Sacred Masculine, and to even become angry at the dominant power that has controlled their lives for so long. Many have felt that adopting Masculine traits was essential if they wanted to succeed in an unfair world, and now struggle to shed the inaccurate belief that the Feminine is inferior to the Masculine. If you have experienced oppression of any form by the Shadow Masculine, or felt forced to manifest his traits in shadow in order to succeed in life, it can be difficult to let go of your preconceptions of what the Sacred Masculine truly is. However, it is impossible to truly embrace the Divine Feminine if you cannot reconcile with the Sacred Masculine.

In order to reconnect to the Divine Feminine, we must first let go of the feelings of anger and resentment aimed at the Sacred Masculine, and understand that it is not his true power that we are rejecting but the Masculine in Shadow. As discussed earlier, the Masculine traits so prized by Western Society are not representative of his strengths, but of his most toxic form. The first thing you must endeavour to do is reject the inaccurate definitions of the Masculine and Feminine that is so prevalent in our culture and be open to the idea that they exist on an interconnected spectrum of divine energy.

The first step in your spiritual journey to reclaim the Divine Feminine is to accept that we are each a unique blend of both masculine and feminine energy, no matter our culture, gender, or societal role. The problems and roadblocks we face in our life do not stem from our tendency to embody either the Divine Feminine or the Sacred Masculine but rather from whether we manifest those traits in light or in shadow. Reject the idea that the Divine Feminine and Sacred Masculine are inherently "good" or "better" than each other, and use meditation, journalling or ritual practice to remind yourself that they are just different aspects of the same Universal Energy, and that both are necessary to becoming an authentic soul.

Take the time to learn about the Sacred Masculine and to consider how it resonates with and complements the Divine Feminine. Ask yourself: do you truly understand the Divine Masculine, or have you only embraced him in the shadow form that is pervasive in the modern world?

Next, review the traits section of this book, and make a list of the Sacred Masculine traits that are twins to the Divine Feminine. As you review each one, think about how they manifest in the real world, and consider people in your life who model those traits. Pay close attention to your emotional reaction to each trait, specifically those that you struggle to picture in anything but a shadow form. These are the ones most likely to hold you back in your quest to accept the duality of Universal power and prevent you from embracing the true power of your core self.

Once you have identified the Sacred Masculine traits that you most struggle with, take the time to study them in your journal and meditate on their true meaning. By all means, start with their shadow forms if that has been your experience, but it is important that you consider how the same trait can be used in a positive form even if you can only think of hypothetical ones to begin with. Once you have completed that task, search out real-world examples of the Sacred Masculine trait being used in light to help reinforce this new perspective.

SACRED MASCULINE TRAIT – EXAMPLE

For example, your experiences of the Sacred Masculine trait of Impassiveness (twin to the Divine Feminine trait of Vulnerability) may have been that those who embody it are emotionally unavailable and unable to build meaningful connections with other people. This is because our society has pushed Impassiveness into shadow, where we have then taught people that crying is childish and that empathy makes you a sucker. At its worst, we discourage people from showing even positive feelings and emotions out of a fear that they will somehow be exploited by others. Men and boys are at particular risk of being harmed by this trait in shadow as we encourage them to repress healthy emotions but then act surprised when that emotion is released in aggressive behaviours or complain when a man is unable to express his feelings articulately. Conversely, women are most likely to be on the receiving end of this aggression and are then criticized if they display the Divine Feminine trait of Vulnerability in either its light or shadow form. On a societal level, Impassiveness in Shadow leads us to victim blame on everything from healthcare to crime, as we are taught to despise vulnerability of any sort as a personal failing. It is no wonder, then, that so many people feel resentful toward the Sacred Masculine if they only see traits in their shadow form.

But what does Impassiveness look like when manifesting in light? What benefits can it possibly bring to both individuals and to society as a whole? Well, Impassiveness is the ability to keep a cool head and remain emotionally detached in stressful situations. It is the ability to keep calm in a crisis and deal only with the problem at hand instead of letting panic overwhelm you. It is an incredibly useful skill for anyone in the emergency services, for surgeons and medical staff, and even for parents when navigating dangerous situations with their children. Whenever there is a crisis underway, it is those who can manifest Impassiveness in light that can step up into leadership and protector roles.

Repeat this process for all of the Sacred Masculine traits and take the time to identify those that you tend to manifest already. Remember that we all are a combination of both Masculine and Feminine traits, but that none of them are inherently wrong or bad. What matters is whether they are manifest in shadow or light, and whether they are utilised in the correct context.

THE SACRED MASCULINE IN RELATIONSHIPS

Here in the Western world, it is common for women to complain that they feel "too masculine" or that they only attract "effeminate partners", and they blame the need to embrace the Sacred Masculine traits to succeed in life for this inability to form meaningful connections.

In truth, this imbalance is usually caused by their adopting the Sacred Masculine in shadow, which has led to them attracting partners who embody their opposite Feminine traits in shadow. Remember that when either the Masculine or the Feminine is in Dominance with the other forced to Submission, their energy can quickly become toxic. Your goal should be to embrace the Divine Feminine that has been suppressed within you, not to eliminate the Divine Masculine from your life.

The key to this process is to accept who you are at present and to be conscious of the traits you utilise the most. As you become increasingly comfortable and confident with the Divine Feminine, it is natural that you will increasingly manifest her traits. At the same time, by making a conscious effort only to embody the Sacred Masculine in light, you will begin the process of reconciling yourself to the knowledge that you are a unique blend of both Masculine and Feminine energies, and that your ideal partner will complement your nature.

It is important to consider that when men are criticized for being "effeminate" and women are criticized for being "too masculine", it is rarely done in reference to the Divine Feminine and Sacred Masculine, but to the gendered norms produced by their society. In the West, women are usually accused of being "masculine" when they demonstrate leadership, occupy positions of authority, or are not afraid to stand up for themselves. Yet the Empress, the Priestess, the Rebel and the Mother are all to be found in positions of power and authority, and none are afraid to lead. It is our society's toxic interpretation of the Sacred Masculine that makes women with authority feel as though they are "too masculine".

Equally, when men are accused of being "effeminate," it is rarely because they embody the Divine Feminine traits of Nurture, Compassion or Forgiveness. In most cases, the term is thrown either at men who are not performative in toxic masculinity – such as the shadow form of Impassiveness discussed in the previous section – or at men who have embraced the shadow side of the Divine Feminine, which we associate with weakness, manipulation and helplessness. In all of these scenarios, the terms Masculine and Feminine are being used to inflict harm, and not with the true understanding that neither is superior to the other, but both are essential to being the best that we can be.

If you are having trouble attracting a suitable partner, first pause to consider how you are interpreting the Divine Feminine and Sacred Masculine, and reflect on whether you have internalised societal models of their shadow forms. Our ideal partners will be a different but complementary blend of the Divine Feminine and Sacred Masculine to that which we manifest, but if you are drawn into shadow, then you will either attract people in shadow to your side or dampen the light of those around you.

17

UTILISING THE DIVINE FEMININE IN EVERYDAY LIFE

SETTING BOUNDARIES & MAINTAINING HEALTHY RELATIONSHIPS

It can be difficult to maintain healthy boundaries with people we care about, and in the West, we are often socially conditioned to prioritize the needs of others above our own. When we regularly suppress our needs and intuition, we lose connection to the warning system that is essential to protecting ourselves and can find ourselves in cycles of unhealthy relationships with parents, partners, friends and colleagues.

Working with the Feminine Archetypes can help you to develop the necessary skills to create healthy boundaries and build successful relationships in all parts of your life. By consciously manifesting the strengths of key archetypes relevant to each situation, you can draw on their power to help you identify the root cause of relationship imbalances and devise an appropriate solution.

Firstly, identify the Archetype that best describes your role in the relationship and whether she is in light or shadow. This will allow you to determine whether you have assumed this archetype by choice or if it has been forced upon you. You can also take the time to uncover whether you have forced another archetype into submission in order to undertake this role.

Next, analyse your feelings about this relationship, particularly the violation of any attempted boundaries, and ask yourself whether the other person is willfully taking advantage of you or if they are doing so out of ignorance. If the former, please be aware that while working with the divine feminine can help you better manage your reactions to this person, you cannot change them or their behaviours. However, you can change your approach to the relationship, which can help you to manage your interactions with the individual. If the latter, you may wish to use the appropriate archetype to instigate a conversation with the person in your life.

Ask yourself what you want to achieve with boundaries or what a healthy relationship with this person would look like – keeping in mind that changes can only be made on your side. Be very clear in your goals when trying to shift the nature of the relationship; do you want to be more explicit in your boundaries? Do you want to express affection in a way that speaks to the other person? Or do you wish to state your needs and expectations in a collaborative manner?

Finally, run through each of the Divine Archetypes in turn and consider the approach they would take to achieving your goals, and how they would interact with the person in your life. This will help you to consider different ways of approaching the issue at hand, allowing you to either dismiss or consider options that you might not otherwise have thought of. When you settle on the best approach for your situation, draw on the strengths of the Divine Feminine traits to help you through the process.

NURTURING INNER CREATIVITY

Modern life in the west can sometimes feel like a rollercoaster where we are constantly on the go. We are bombarded by entertainment options so that boredom is never an option, but still never seem to have enough time to do everything we want to do. Unfortunately, it seems that indulging our creativity and passion is the first thing we let go of when we are running out of time.

This is a mistake. Creation is a key part of the human existence, and it needs to be indulged in order to grow. If you are struggling to come up with creative solutions to problems you face in work and in life, it is likely because you have stopped being creative in your free time. It is not uncommon for people with hectic work lives to feel as though they need to be 100% productive and produce results from every activity, and sadly the Western world reinforces this unobtainable ideal in us. We strive for perfection, almost always fail to achieve this impossible standard, and then proceed to berate ourselves for failing to reach the unachievable goal we set for ourselves in the first place.

And yet, whatever it is you wish to achieve in your life – be that spiritual fulfilment, a meaningful career, or to make a positive difference in the world – you will not achieve it if you keep doing the same things that have led you to your current point in life. Solutions and changes cannot be found without creativity, and like everything else we need to succeed in life, creativity is a skill that needs to be developed, and not a trait people are born with.

If you wish to be creative, you need to let go of the idea of perfection and give yourself permission to be terrible at something. This may sound counter-intuitive, especially if you are a high-achiever, but no one starts out in life being able to do anything perfectly. We must crawl before we can walk, but before we can even crawl, we must learn to turn over and move our limbs independently. Your first attempts at anything will likely be failures, but that is not a bad thing. Arguably, the Wright brothers built some of the worst aeroplanes in existence, but had they not been willing to learn from their mistakes and be pleased when they finally got something to fly, we would not have modern air travel or space flight.

Once you are able to accept that doing something badly is part of the journey, it is time to bring the Creator into dominance, and remember to practice the basics, try new things, and never to let your failures and disappointments prevent you from trying to create something new.

While you are learning to indulge your creativity, it is important to look outside of your own field for inspiration and innovation. Crochet and knitting has led to innovations in medical science, while creative writing led us to space flight. We communicate important messages through visual media, while music has been used to influence society since our first ancestors learned how to sing. It is important to realise that your creativity should not be limited to one narrow field or focus if you truly want to maximise its potential; do not feel guilty for indulging more than one outlet for your imagination, for it is often through exploring different artistic endeavours that we find solutions to the problems we are facing.

Finally, keep your heart open to new experiences and your mind open to the innovations of others. It is not possible for any one person to be at the cutting edge of every field out there, so choose those that most interest you or are the most relevant to your core passions, and approach them with the wide-eyed wonder of the Maiden and the spirit of the adventurer. Sometimes when it feels like your own creativity is stuck or stunted, allowing yourself to be impressed by the innovations of others will provide the fuel for your own inspiration.

MANIFESTATION AND THE DIVINE FEMININE

Even the newest of practitioners to spiritual practice have heard of Manifestation, and it is often suggested to those who are frustrated with their current circumstances as a way to bring abundance into their lives. Manifestation is one of the most powerful tools available to help people become the best version of themselves, and yet it is also one of the most misunderstood. It is often sold to people as "if you believe in it hard enough, then it will happen," leading to unrealistic expectations and disappointment when a landslide of cheques doesn't arrive magically in their mailbox.

But just because people incorrectly use the tool does not mean that it is useless. If you are willing to put in the work to learn the Manifestation process, then it can produce significant results in your life.

What is Manifestation?

While visualisation and the setting of intentions are both parts of Manifestation, the process is not as simple as many people would have you believe. Rather, it is about becoming the architect of your own life, and being the driving force behind the creation of your own future.

The good news is that you are already doing this, albeit on a subconscious level. Every decision you make, every reaction you have, moves you along a path toward your future, whether you like it or not. Manifestation is simply the act of taking this to a conscious level, so that you can influence the direction your life will take.

The less good news is that using Manifestation correctly is difficult and time-consuming. It is important to acknowledge right from the start that Manifestation is a real-world process that takes time, effort and energy. It is not a magical spell that will bring you abundance or fix your problems overnight. You cannot use Manifestation to demand wealth or opportunity from the Divine Feminine or the Universal Energy in general, for they do not exist to indulge your whims, nor can they be commanded to change the world to your liking. Here in the West, we exist in a Capitalist society that is characterised by an uneven playing field and a multitude of unseen, uncontrollable forces that can derail even the best-laid plans. You can visualise the most perfect future imaginable with no pain or suffering for anyone, but reality will ensure that it never comes to pass. You cannot control the actions of others, stop natural disasters, or cheat death no matter how hard you try.

So if you cannot control your future with Manifestation, why bother with it at all?

Why practice Manifestation?

While Manifestation cannot change reality, it does provide you with the tools to influence the direction of your life. Imagine that you are lost and alone in a vast forest; every decision that you take will lead you either toward or away from your survival, and the tools you have at your disposal will further influence your ability to thrive. Most people make the decision just to wander about aimlessly and just hope for the best – this is the equivalent to subconscious manifestation – and react to the immediate threats they encounter from their environment. A lucky few will survive and do well from this process, but most will remain lost, afraid, and make reactive decisions to survive as long as possible.

Some will deny the reality of their situation and convince themselves that they are not lost and that the environment is not hostile. They make no effort to find a way out of the forest, but instead close their eyes and just wish as hard as they can that they were safe at home instead of in the wilderness. When the dangers of the wild catch up with them, they are unprepared and only move forward when running away from the threats that have found them. This is the equivalent of toxic positivity masquerading as Manifestation; these practitioners wish for a magical solution while denying the reality of their situation.

The final group takes the time to try and work out where they are and how they got there in the first place. They have tools for navigation at their disposal, and do their best to understand the potential dangers of their environment. They have plans to deal with any problems that they face before they happen, and while they know they may not be able to overcome every obstacle in their path, they can use their maps to find an alternative route around them. This group knows the direction they need to go to get to their destination, even if they cannot locate the path. While they face the same unexpected dangers as the other groups do, they are the best equipped to survive them, and even turn them to their advantage. This is the equivalent of conscious Manifestation; it acknowledges the reality of the now and the threats that are outside of our control, but maximises the chances of success with clear goals, preparation, and determination.

Done properly, Manifestation helps you navigate the real world so that you achieve greater abundance, success and happiness than you would if you simply let life happen to you. The more you practice and commit to the process, the greater the potential for your future.

Using the Divine Feminine in the Manifestation process

The Divine Feminine archetypes are an excellent tool to help you at all stages of the Manifestation process, from deciding what it is you truly want to create in your life to navigating the twists and turns that life may throw at you.

If you are new to Manifestation, the easiest place to start is by allowing yourself to daydream. Draw on the Adventurer and the Creator to help you become excited about the potential and possibility for your future. This is the one stage where you do not have to let reality limit your dreams, so indulge your imagination and enjoy the process!

Keep notes in your journal about the common themes and images that turn up in your daydreams. Invoke the Priestess and her intuition or the Lover and her passion to help you determine which of these things represent what you truly want, as opposed to those you think you should desire. For example, it is not uncommon for people starting out on the Manifestation process to concentrate on material gains like designer clothing or luxury cars, but when they finally get them, they discover very little joy in the ownership of these items. This is usually because we as a culture are indoctrinated into believing that we need socially acceptable displays of wealth in order to be truly successful instead of focussing on what we truly desire in our souls.

This part of the process can be surprisingly difficult and trying to separate what you truly want from what you feel that you deserve can lead you to uncover buried traumas and unhelpful behaviours. If this happens to you, do not be afraid to seek out professional support and therapy to help you work through any deep-seated issues that have been impacting your behaviours on a subconscious level, for the best thing you can do for yourself is begin to heal.

Once you have identified the main things you want to manifest in your life, it is time to bring the Scholar into the mix. Use her skills to research the feasibility of your goals, and to help you outline the necessary steps you will need to take to bring those them to reality. For example, if you desire to travel, you should research the countries you wish to visit, visa requirements, costs, whether you want a resort stay or to go off the beaten track, and so on. In some cases, you may find that your dreams are not obtainable due to reasons outside of your control, but this provides you with the opportunity to find similar, adjacent opportunities for fulfilment.

The next part of the manifestation process is to break down the path from your current reality to your desired goals into a series of manageable steps. After all, you are not going to be able to walk on the moon without becoming an astronaut, but being an astronaut will require both physical and educational standards to be met first. Your goals might not be quite so lofty but knowing the steps necessary to achieve them is essential if you want them to be more than dreams. The Empress can be of great help as you develop your plan, for her ability to bring order from chaos and develop workable solutions to get you from where you are right now to where you want to be in the most practical way possible.

This phase is also the perfect time to identify any potential threats that could derail your progress toward goals and to acknowledge them within your planning process. Your goal may be to build your own home and sanctuary, but if you plan to place it in an area prone to earthquakes or extreme weather, then the design of your future property will have to take these things into account, as will the amount of money you set aside for insurance, or you may have to consider alternative locations. Tap into your inner Hunter to help you through this stage of the process, for she understands that the world can be dangerous and knows how to plan for the worst while hoping for the best.

It is important to remember, however, that even the best-laid plans can be derailed by real-world events outside of your control. Do not be afraid to change your goals or plan steps in the face of changing circumstances; our reality is a dynamic, ever-changing flow of energy, and we must be prepared to navigate those changes even when we are not sure where they will take us.

The final stage of the Manifestation Process is to take action. Using your plan as a guide, work toward implementing each step so that you make progress toward your goal, no matter how small those steps may happen to be. There will be times when you grow frustrated with the speed of your progress and feel like you are not seeing benefits fast enough for your liking, but invoke the grace of the Archetypes and accept that this process is long, hard work, and challenging. Regularly take the time to review your progress, and actively remind yourself that even the smallest of positive changes will lead to major results in the long term.

FINAL THOUGHTS ON MANIFESTATION

Whether you are new to Manifestation or have been practising for years, it is good to remind yourself of the limitations of this process and to be sure that the things you are trying to manifest are within your power to create. You do not have the power to compel other people to change their behaviours or the ability to change their emotions. You cannot change the weather or natural phenomenon. You cannot influence the markets, the lottery, or the casino, and you definitely cannot change the past no matter how much you wish to. It is easy to slip from Manifestation to Wishful Thinking, but by being thoughtful, reflective and intentional in your goal-setting and planning processes, you should be able to avoid this common pitfall.

THE DIVINE FEMININE AS GODDESS WORSHIP

Women have been rulers, changemakers, scientists, philosophers and religious leaders throughout history, although it is only recently that our society has sought to reclaim and celebrate these narratives. In the same way, interest has been renewed in the role played by Goddesses in both the spiritual and societal world, and it has become common to see celebrities invoking goddess imagery in their works. These have not always been successfully executed, and accusations of appropriation and fetishization are not uncommon.

It is not surprising. For those of us brought up in the Abrahamic religions or in secular societies, the concept of goddess worship can feel strange or even exotic in nature, when it is actually us who are the cultural outliers on this issue. In our enthusiasm to embrace the Feminine Divine, we can forget that she has always been here and that she has always been celebrated by other cultures and religions, and that we do not have the right to snatch at her like greedy children before we have undertaken the work and study necessary to be respectful and open in her light.

For some, choosing a goddess to relate to is approached like a magazine horoscope reading or an internet quiz. At best, these tools present generic responses drawn from a limited range of deities, while at worst, they can perpetuate harmful stereotypes and promote ignorance of living spiritual practices. Nonetheless, these internet quizzes are often the first exposure many of us have to the idea of selecting a patron goddess, which is why they remain so popular.

It is understandable that, after growing up in a culture starved of the Divine Feminine, we reach out blindly for her influence and demand our place at her altar. Still, such behaviour does not help us to manifest her traits and only drives us further from understanding. Too often, we take the name or the image of a goddess and shape her into what we think the Feminine Divine should be with little thought to the complex nature of her existence in the culture that manifested her in the first place. We forget that we are the students in this process and that our shadow Masculine society has warped our perceptions of what the Divine Feminine is and should be. This is where accusations of fetishization and appropriation are valid, for how can we claim to be honouring the Divine Feminine in goddess form if we do not understand what aspects and traits the goddess herself personifies?

As part of your studies to understand and embrace the Divine Feminine, it is essential to learn about how goddess worship forms part of the belief systems of past and present cultures. The worship of female deities can be traced back over 27,000 years, and there are countless figurines and votive offerings depicting women found across all time periods and all cultures. Our levels of knowledge about specific deities can vary considerably depending on how well past civilisations have been recorded and debated, but nonetheless, there is a wealth of material and information out there for you to learn from.

When it comes to goddesses that are worshipped by modern societies around the world, it is important to learn from her worshippers directly wherever possible. Too often, we make assumptions about the beliefs of others because it is impossible to understand the world outside of our own cultural bias. By opening ourselves to the light and being respectful in our quest to learn, we can eliminate the risk of appropriation and fetishization of the goddesses we seek to connect with, and engage with other cultures in a humble, considerate manner.

Wherever you live in the world, as part of your spiritual practice, take the time to learn about the traditional beliefs and cultures that existed there in the past. These may have gone through several iterations and pantheons over the years but learning about how those who lived there before you worshipped and connected to the land will heighten your own insight and inform your spiritual practice. Be mindful and respectful of the deities that were worshipped there, and be especially humble when interacting with existing belief systems and/or descendants of marginalised/displaced populations.

Finally, it is essential to remember that while goddesses are a manifestation of the Divine Feminine, they are also shaped by the culture and beliefs of the society that first worshipped them. This means that goddesses who seem to represent the same concept - such as Love, Harvest, War, or Childbirth – can be wildly different in terms of the traits and archetypes they embody. Take the goddesses of Love as a prime example: The Greek Goddess Aphrodite is not synonymous with the Egyptian Goddess Hathor, nor is the Hindu Goddess Lakshmi identical to the Nordic Goddess Freyja. Choosing the wrong goddess as a channel for the Feminine Divine can lead you to manifest traits or archetypes that are not in line with your goals, which in turn can lead to unforeseen and even negative consequences. Equally, the forms of worship associated with each goddess will also impact your spiritual practice. Some require sacrifices and gifts, others respond to prayers, and yet others are traditionally bargained with. While we are used to the idea of a deity that is omnipresent, it is also important to ascertain whether the goddess you are drawn to is all-pervading or if her powers are tied to specific locations and places. Of course, there is nothing stopping you from worshipping any deity you choose in any manner you like but be clear with yourself that this action is not a true spiritual connection with the goddess in question; you are merely appropriating her name or image to embody a concept of your own choosing.

Connecting with a goddess on a spiritual level only happens through study, understanding, ritual and practice. The transformation you seek through connection to the Divine Feminine requires research, work, and commitment but will ultimately impact you more than a shallow spiritual practice based on misunderstandings and appropriation. The Divine Feminine has been worshipped through goddesses throughout human history and continues to this day; learn from those with more experience than you, and eventually, you will find those true connections for yourself.

To help you begin your studies into the practice of goddess worship, here is a list of female deities for you to research and consider alongside those you may already be familiar with. Remember to seek original sources wherever possible and to examine all aspects of the goddess, including the rituals and nature of her worship. To take your study to a deeper level, take the time to learn about the entire pantheon of gods and goddesses that your subject is a part of, as well as exploring the culture and society of both their original and current worshippers.

The list includes goddesses from ancient Semitic, Welsh, Haitian, Norse, Egyptian, Māori, Aztec, Maya, Japanese Buddhist, Hopi, Hindu, Chinese, Lithuanian, and Yoruba cultures. Each of these goddesses embodies a unique and powerful aspect of feminine energy, and their stories and attributes offer a rich source of inspiration for women seeking to tap into their own divine feminine energy. Whether seeking guidance on motherhood, prosperity, love, or transformation, the goddesses on this list offer a powerful and diverse range of archetypes and symbols to help women connect with their own inner strength and wisdom.

AFTERWORD

As you continue your journey to reclaim the Divine Feminine, remember that every one of us, regardless of culture, gender, identity or social status, embodies and expresses her aspects in one way or another. Even though we have allowed our society to suppress and wound her power, she is never truly gone or destroyed, for she is as essential to existence as the Divine Masculine.

Your quest is to reclaim an essential part of your nature that is not so much lost as buried. It is on you to shed the cultural judgements of good/bad, clean/unclean, pride/shame that we have all been taught about the interplay of masculine and feminine energies and to appreciate them both as the essential powers they are.

It will not be easy. You will have to unlearn much you have been taught as Truth and live with the discomfort of challenging and changing your harmful beliefs. There will be times when you want to race through the work and declare your development complete rather than accepting that you will be discovering new knowledge and perspectives for the rest of your existence.

It will not be quick. While this book is designed to be an introduction to three core aspects of the Divine Feminine – Traits, Goddesses, and Archetypes – there is a wealth of information and discourse on each of these topics out there, and there are as many different interpretations of the Divine Feminine as there are belief systems in the world. The goal is to find the ones that make sense to you while understanding why meaning is found elsewhere by other people. Approach your journey with humility and respect, and you will find your strength and purpose as the Divine Feminine welcomes you home.

Printed in Great Britain
by Amazon